MEAN

i: u didnt know that?

: no way!

i: where have u been

NICE SHIRT

DIET MUCH

AYSOS?

GIRLS

U-G-L-Y

MEAN GIRLS

FACING YOUR BEAUTY TURNED BEAST

HAYLEY DIMARCO

Revell
a division of Baker Publishing Group
Grand Rapids, Michigan

Hungry Planet

Library of Congress Cataloging-in-Publication Data
DiMarco, Hayley.
    Mean girls : facing your beauty turned beast / Hayley DiMarco.—Rev. and updated.
        p.   cm.
    ISBN 978-0-8007-3293-6 (pbk.)
    1. Teenage girls—Psychology. 2. Christian teenagers—Psychology.
3. Interpersonal relations in adolescence. I. Title.
    BF724.D56 2008
    248.8′33—dc22   2008018384

Published in association with Yates & Yates, LLP, Literary Agents, Orange, California.

CON-
TENTS

The Spiritual Side of Mean

Fighting Mean

Ending Mean

THE BEAST

The Mean Girl. The beast. The one who tears at your flesh and devours your heart. She growls when you walk by. She hisses as you leave. She probably drools in her sleep at the thought of tormenting you. She's a beast, all right, plain and simple. It's evident in all she is and all she does. So what do you do with this beast in your life? Can you find a hint of hope, or are you destined to spend your life running in fear from this rabid female? Oh, my dear, the answer is near. Come with me on a journey through the bizarre and the twisted. Join me in scrutinizing the female psyche, and follow me to a land of freedom and hope.

Girls have become the most catty, manipulative, emotional people on the planet, and you are at their mercy. Or are you? At one time I didn't see a way out, so weak was my faith. But now I do. I believe that the Mean Girl can be a thing of the past. I believe that her power over you will diminish and that your victories will be many. Your bruises will heal and your cuts will mend. *Mean Girls* is a call to spiritual strength. A call to stand firm. It is a call to face the beasts in your life head on and with faithful resolve. And it is the answer that you've been looking for. Mean Girls . . . shall we attempt to find the beauty in your beast?

MY STORY

If you have a Mean Girl in your life, I understand more than you might know how horrible you feel right now. You hate getting up in the morning because you know that as soon as you get to school or work, she will be there. Leering at you, laughing at you, thinking about you, *talking* about you. You don't know what she'll do next or where she will be. Oh yes, I know that feeling all too well because my high school years were plagued with Mean Girls.

In my small class of forty people, I was the victim of choice for the popular crowd. For four years I hated going to school. I sat in class day in and day out and watched them plot and plan to hurt me. I tried to make friends, but in the end even they turned against me in one way or another. The kiss of death for me (which might have some of you rolling your eyes) was that all the boys liked me. I was really shy, and so I guess I was kind of mysterious. I also wasn't a sexually active girl, so, boys being boys, they all wanted to get the virgin. (News flash: they failed miserably!)

I was continually the subject of all kinds of plots. If I was dating a guy, they wanted to get him from me. If I had a nice car, they wanted to ruin the paint job. If my mom trusted me, they wanted her to stop trusting me. One day a pair of panties was placed in our mailbox as if someone was returning them to me after a night of passion. What a joke. Torturing me was quite a sport for them, though. Every day when I left school I would find a big wad of spit on the hood of my car. Every day, without fail. I hated walking out to my car as they all laughed at me. I can remember being afraid to go to the bathroom because I might meet one of them in there alone, and that would be devastating.

When I started dating a guy that one of them wanted to date, they not only TP'd his house but also spray painted his driveway with bad things about *me*. They were bent on making me look bad.

When our Sadie Hawkins dance (girls ask guys) came along, one of the girls asked my boyfriend before I could (of course, he was a stupid boy for saying yes, but that's beside the current point).

I thought I had found sanctuary in those few friends I told you about, but they soon turned on me as well. Why is it that girls think that boys are more important than their friends? My friend made out with my new crush the day after he and I found each other. I was shocked, but I guess I shouldn't have been. After all, friends aren't as important as boys. Ugh!

All this meanness finally culminated in one horrible act that freaked me out and made me fear for my safety. One day during my senior year I went to my locker, and as I opened it I saw a small noose with something hanging from it. It was soft and slimy like a dead finger. A note that hung from the rope said, "Beware the DOA." Needless to say, it totally freaked me out. I slammed the locker and ran to the school office. This was too much. Until that time I hadn't said anything to anyone, but this looked like something that should be taken more seriously.

When the principal went back to check my locker, she found that what was hanging there was a peeled carrot, carved to look like a person. Apparently it had been left in the freezer overnight so that now it was cold, clammy, and limp. Pretty ingenious, even for Mean Girls!

I was devastated that their hatred of me had gone that far. I don't know for sure why the girls decided that I was archenemy number one, but I was. Was it because I was shy? Was I aloof in my shyness? I'll never know, but my high school years were tainted by the treatment of a handful of angry teenage girls.

I always thought they had no idea what they were doing to me—until years later when I found out the truth. I was at a party with a bunch of friends from high school, and one of the Mean Girls was there too. She pulled me aside and said, "We treated you really bad in school and did some really mean things. I'm sorry about what we did." I thought that was a really nice and noble thing to do, so I smiled and said, "Oh, don't worry about it. We were young; it's okay. I forgive you." She looked at me in shock, her mouth open, and said, "Oh, great. Why'd you have to be so nice even now? It would have been much easier if you would have been mean about it!" Even then, my kindness was driving her nuts. Maybe that's what they mean by "kill 'em with kindness."

I didn't learn to trust girls until years after high school. I spent most of my college and adult life, up until a few years ago, only being close to guys. I just couldn't handle the "girl scene," as I liked to call it. "They are just so catty and mean. I don't like 'em. Guys are easygoing, not vindictive or petty. I prefer guys," I used to say. But now that I have healed from my experiences and started to see the truth, I can say that I love girls. In fact, I *need* girls. If it weren't for girls, I would be really messed up. Let's face it, we need each other. Guys are great, sure, but they are different, and you can't really connect with a guy the same way you can connect with a girl.

Now I can sit up all night with my girlfriends, talking about life. I can talk their ears off and never feel like I'm boring them. I can shop all day with my girlfriends. I can share clothes with them. Tell my secrets to them. Confide in them. And nurture them. Girls bring out the girl in me, and that's pretty cool. Because when you get right down to it, it's the girl in you that guys are attracted to, not the guy in you. I didn't understand that till many years after high school. I was so busy trying not to be like the Mean Girls that I became like a guy and totally gave up my girlyness. And it wasn't until I decided I really wanted a man and was ready to think of the "M" word that I found out I really needed girls.

So what I'm saying is that guys will never replace girls. They weren't meant to. Most guys don't need to talk as much as girls, so we need backup friends to use all our words on. Guys, on the whole, don't like shopping as much either, so we need girls to fill that void. And most guys definitely don't like sharing all their hopes, fears, and emotions with us all the time like we want to, but girls do, and I thank God for that. My mom always told me, "Hayley, whenever you start dating someone, don't stop seeing your girlfriends. You need them. If you dump them and expect him to take their place, you'll be in big trouble. He just can't do it. He's a guy. Save all your girl emotions and traumas for girls who get it. And just enjoy the guy." Women who are wise know that even after you get married, keeping your girlfriends is essential. Guys and girls both need "me" time, and a girlfriend is a good sounding board and confidante for your emotions and dreams.

So don't give up on girls just yet. We have fun together. We bond in ways guys never can. And besides, you need someone to get your back, to tell you when your jeans are too short or your belt doesn't match your shoes or, worse yet, when you have something in your teeth. Ah, girls. They are great. Don't let a few mean ones taint it for the rest of us. Find a girlfriend or two and make a good relationship that will last a lifetime.

When I was a teenager, my spirit was imprisoned by fear, maybe like yours is right now. I had no sense of the greatness of God or the power of his hand in my life. I couldn't see life from his point of view, only from my weak little place on the planet. I didn't understand a bigger picture because I had not yet discovered Christ and his teachings, his Spirit, and his love. I didn't come to understand that until after college. If I had known *then* what I know *now*, maybe those girls would have ended up my friends, or at least left me alone a little bit. No one ever told me how to handle them, what to say to them, or how to be around them. Instead I was just plain scared of them. I lived a lot of my life in fear, and it didn't have to be that way. How sad that no one was there to tell me about the amazing truth of godliness with love. Now that I have come through years of fighting with the Mean Girl and of not knowing how to avoid her or get rid of her, I have a new understanding of how I am supposed to react to her, even if I can't get rid of her.

I wrote Mean Girls to help you better understand who you are so that you can stop the Mean Girl cycle. This book will help you to find your destiny and live in it as a graceful spiritual girl. Mean Girls will help you face the beauty in the beast of your Mean Girl and maybe even find a way to change a generation of Mean Girls from the inside out. What you learn in this book might shock you. It might even tick you off, but don't stop. If you want to get to the bottom of your pain, then you have to power through. On the other side are hope and a life filled with peace and love. Mean Girls might be around you forever, but they might never affect you again if you follow the principles in this book and remain honest with, and true to, yourself.

WHY THIS BOOK WORKS

This book contains some powerful stuff that is guaranteed to help you with the Mean Girl(s) in your life if you are willing to live by it. This isn't for the faint of heart. It isn't self-help for the brave or the strong. It's about a way of life based on the truth offered by a best-selling book called the Bible. Conquering the mean in your life is only going to work if you have a power bigger than yourself working alongside you, above you, and in you. And I hope that by the end of this book you will know a little bit more about this life-changing power that tramples mean. So be warned: you might find some tips and tricks in here that make perfect sense and try to do them, and life might get a little bit better, but without faith in a God who can change lives and change hearts, any change will only be temporary. So let's dive into the realm of mean and see if we can't find real beauty.

THE MEAN GIRL QUIZ

Do you have a Mean Girl problem?
Answer the following to find out.

1. When you walk down the hall, most of the time you are:
   (a) alone
   (b) with your gang
   (c) with your best bud

2. Sometimes you:
   (a) get laughed at by other girls
   (b) make fun of the not-so-popular girl's clothes
   (c) hang with your friends and have so much fun you forget it's time to go

3. You know how it feels to:
   (a) be gossiped about
   (b) make someone look bad so you look good
   (c) care for a friend who is hurt

4. You spend hours:
   (a) worrying about how not to be seen by other girls
   (b) thinking about how to get even with someone
   (c) helping your friends through tough times

5. When you go to school you are:
   (a) afraid to go to the bathroom alone
   (b) lovin' life
   (c) counseling your friends about all their problems

6. Your parents:
   (a) would say you worry a lot about going to school
   (b) know that you are happiest when you are with your friends
   (c) taught you how to care for others

7. At least once a week:
   (a) another girl laughs at you or picks on you
   (b) you talk about another girl in a way that puts her down
   (c) you try to make your friend feel really good about herself

8. You have cried at school:
   (a) many times
   (b) only occasionally when a guy is a jerk
   (c) hardly ever, because you save that for your bedroom

Now add up your scores:

(a) = 3
(b) = 2
(c) = 1

18–24: MG problems. You probably have to deal with at least one girl who is out to get you. This book will help you learn more about her and how to handle yourself when she freaks out on you. Don't worry, this won't last forever. This trauma you are living in has an end. Keep the faith.

11–17: MG. Did you ever think that you might be the Mean Girl of someone's nightmares? This quiz isn't a perfect diagnosis, but you might want to read on to find out who you are when others are looking.

8–10: No MG for you. You probably are the one helping the victims of MGs. You see the pain they cause but have mostly stayed free from their attacks. You'll be in a great place if you can learn more about them so you can help more than you do right now. You are the key to solving the troubles between these girls. Never stop being faithful.

MEAN GIRLS—
WHO ARE THEY?

TWO KINDS OF MEAN

In my estimation there are two kinds of Mean Girls, each with their own set of hassles. **The first one is the Really Mean Girl who is mean for fun, and she is just plain misery on legs.** And the second one is Mean for a Reason. Usually what makes them different is their motivation—why they do the mean they do. Let's start off with the Really Mean Girl.

You see her at the other end of the hall. Your stomach rolls over and thinks about climbing up your throat. **The Really Mean Girl. The one whose job it is to torture you.** As you walk closer, she begins to whisper to her friends while she stares at you. They giggle and all look at you at once. The humiliation brings the blood to your cheeks. If only you could hide the pain, but it's out there for all to see. As you walk past them, you pull your books in to your chest for protection. You feel the sharp pain of knives driving into your back, and you wince. What have you done? Why do they hate you? What will they do next? And who will believe them?

Really Mean Girls define themselves based on who they can hurt. It's a power trip.

A third of all girls surveyed said they had been too afraid to go to school at some point in their lives.

Their goal in life. It gives them satisfaction to see you squirm. It makes them feel good when you get mad at them. And it makes them look good to all their friends when they point out how pathetic you are. They don't need any other reason. It's not what you've done; it's how really mean they've become. Their mean is just for fun.

But the second Mean Girl is a little less obvious. She's a nice girl gone bad. Or worse yet, a best friend gone ballistic. She is the girl who is **Mean for a Reason**. She sees something you did as a direct attack on her, and because of that, she's after you. Revenge is her middle name, and she'll do all she can to settle the score. This kind of girl can be nice to everyone else, and that can make it worse, because not everyone sees her subtle jabs or her silent attacks. But you do, and you want them gone. But this girl feels justified, and only proving that you are the bad girl will make her feel any better. She's just a girl who believes she has been wronged and is only seeking to "fix things." I'd say that most mean girls fit into this category.

Truth be told, if you have ever uttered the words "But she started it!" then very possibly you are being mean for a reason. And reason or not, mean is mean.

Getting even isn't all you think it is. It isn't a way to rid the world of Mean Girls. And it isn't the quickest way to happiness and freedom from Little Miss Meany. In fact, it's the exact opposite: when you get even, you are really giving the other girl power over you. And you have taken the first step in shaping your heart into one just like hers. Getting even means getting her in your system. You know how it feels. She becomes your obsession. You think about her all day. You plot. You talk. You plan. She's in your head all the time. Ick! The very girl you detest is now in charge of your actions.

The truth is, when you get even, you lose. Doesn't seem

fair, does it? Self-protection seems like your right but that's not true. Your job is to obey God no matter what the world throws at you. And God's commands are the exact opposite of what your Mean Girl is trying to get out of you. Don't let her dig so deep into your soul that she removes truth and replaces it with hatred and loathing. Those are not God's plans for your heart and mind.

TWO DIFFERENT FIGHTS

These two kinds of Mean Girls are different creatures, and how you choose to deal with them will make a world of difference.

The Really Mean Girl who is mean for fun is your toughest opponent, and fighting her is usually a no-win situation. Girls who are mean for fun are operating on an entirely different set of values than the rest of the world. And convincing them of anything that might make them lay off of you will be very difficult if not impossible. Their sole focus in life is to destroy others; they don't have to have a reason why. And for some, this thirst might even at times turn violent. She's not someone to play with, and your best bet is to steer clear of her and learn the lesson that you don't have the power to change anyone but yourself. The Really Mean Girl defies most of the self-help advice available on the topic of mean. But that doesn't mean there's no hope, because losing the mean in your life is also up to you. She might not make a change, but you surely can. And it's how you choose to *react to* the Really Mean Girl that will determine how mean affects you.

The girl who is Mean for a Reason, on the other hand, might be a more hopeful case. She is a girl just like you and me who is just a little off track, a little self-obsessed, and she's making your life miserable. She might be an acquaintance, a friend, or even a family member. And because of that her mean hits very close to home. Fortunately, the girl who is Mean for a Reason has a sense of justice and morality that is simply misguided, and that means helping her to see the light and change is a much more feasible possibility. If you have a girl in your life who might be Mean for a Reason, then there are some things that you can do and say that just might make a world of difference in your relationship. But either way, the work that you really have to do when faced with a Mean Girl is internal. Mean Girls can only hurt you as badly as you allow them to. So let's start to work on you and your Mean Girl problem.

THE MEAN GIRL'S GOAL

The number one goal of the Mean Girl is to inflict pain. To her and her cohorts, your pain is evidence of her victory. So in the game of mean, your pain is her point. And just like in any other game, the person with the most points wins. So your goal should be to make sure you don't give her any points. In other words, never let her see your pain. Anything that you do in response to her mean (other than something loving) will show her that she got to you and injured you, and *cha-ching!* Her point.

So how do you hide your pain so that she doesn't get a point? Well, it's a funny thing about pain, especially emotional pain: it's unnoticeable to others unless you choose to express it. In other words, they have no idea how you feel on the inside until you show them or tell them. Every time you get mad, cry, yell, shout, run away, retaliate, or do anything else in response to your pain,

> When anyone provokes you, remember that it is your own opinion about him that provokes you. Try not to be tossed around by appearances.
>
> —Epectitus

you've just let her get a glimpse of your insides and all the pain she's caused, and the point goes to the Mean Girl.

Unfortunately for most, our first instinct when being attacked is always to protect ourselves. It's the old fight or flight thing. Someone swings, and you automatically cover your face. The same is true for mean: someone lashes out at you with words, and your first response will be to protect yourself. But believe me when I say that your instinct is counterproductive. In the long run it does nothing for you and everything for your Mean Girl. Sure, speaking your mind feels really good in the moment, but then you have to live with the aftershocks.

You see, mean is a living, breathing thing that grows and grows the more it's fed. It lives off the attention of girls just like you, loving your pain, your anger, and your retaliation. All those reactions just give mean a reason to live. Without them, what good is the attack? They need to see blood; they need to see pain; they want to know you are in agony. It gives mean wings. So if you want to put a stranglehold on mean, then you have to cut off its life force—your negative reaction.

You just can't let the Mean Girl see you sweat. Your nonplussed reaction might not get her to stop immediately, or ever, but if you let her see your pain, then you've given her a point, and it's game on! So don't let her get any points on you. At home, alone in your room, or with your family, you can break down and let it all out, but do all you can in the presence of the Mean Girl or others who will report back to her to stay calm and loving. Any sign of pain is a sign of weakness, and that, unfortunately, is a green light for more mean.

Listen, the most important thing to learn in a life of dealing with mean is that you can't really control or change the life of any other person but yourself. All the yelling, scheming, and hating in the world won't make her nicer or make her go away. That instinct of self-protection that causes you to retaliate or even to show that she got a point only fuels her fire. So if you've tried out this cycle of mean in the past and you don't like where it's gotten you, why not try another approach? I always say, if you keep doing what you're doing, you're going to keep getting what you've got. Is that enough?

If your answer is no, that's not enough—I don't like the status quo—then you came to the right place. Because in this book you aren't going to read about tactics to avenge yourself or to smear another girl or ways you can prove to the world that all she says and does is wrong. No, this book is more realistic, and the goal isn't to give you some kind of false hope that you have the power to control everything everyone says and does to you, because you don't. The goal of this book is to teach you to see the Mean Girl and yourself through the eyes of God. You'll also learn how he expects you to manage yourself in the midst of mean and how his expectations actually save you in ways far superior to the world's ideas of self-protection and fighting back.

WHY ME?

When it comes to your Mean Girl, do you ever ask, *"Why me, God?"* I know I did. And I struggled with that question for years, long after school was over and done with. When I started working in the corporate world, I found out girls were just as bad there as in school. Conniving, backstabbing, and manipulative, only this time they had real power over me. Unfortunately, big girls can be just as mean as younger girls. You think they will go away or just get more mature, but they never do. So why do you think you can't get rid of Mean Girls? What is God's reason for allowing them in our lives? After all, nothing happens without his okay. He's the boss, the real boss. So what's up with Mean Girls? *"Why, God, why?"*

"Why not?" just might be his response. Why are you so surprised when bad things happen to you, as if the world were outside of the influence of the power of darkness? (Read 1 Peter 4:12 and 1 John 5:19–20.) Why are you asking God "Why?" rather than asking "How should I respond to another's actions?" After all, should we be questioning God (see Isaiah 45:11)? Why not ask him instead, "What do you want me to learn from this?"

As you read through this book, you will find things you can do that might help you ease the pain caused by the Mean Girl and might even ease her pain. But before you get to that, you have to realize that the most important thing is how *you* change because of this, not whether or not *she* changes. After all, you are ultimately the only one you can control. How will your faith grow and how will you become a stronger and better person because of this girl's actions? Are you going to choose to let her win in your life, or God? This Mean Girl might be your chance to really live your faith, to put feet to what you say you believe. She is a living opportunity to infuse God's Word into your life. Wow, who knew she could be so valuable to you? It's like this: How do you prove your perseverance and faithfulness to God if you have nothing to persevere through? How do you grow in character if you have no trials to overcome? This girl is your lotto ticket to building character. It might not seem like it now, but if you trust him, really trust him, then you have to know that what others intend for evil, God intends for good (see Genesis 50:20).

So what kind of spiritual good is coming your way if you are open to the idea that God can use even this Mean Girl to better your life? Well, several things can happen in the life of a believer who suffers. Let's take a look.

PURIFICATION

One of the big reasons God allows trials and junk in your life is to purify you. It's like that refiner's fire everyone always talks about—the fire that burns all the impurities out of gold and keeps all the good parts of it. You have to be purified, and purification takes place in extreme ways, like fires (see 1 Peter 1:7) and Mean Girls. So if she is your refiner's fire, what will your reaction be? Will you fight against your refining and jump out of the fire meant to make you pure? Or will you turn to God and say, "What shall I become for you?" If you can learn to act the way God calls you to act in the face of the Mean Girl, then you will get closer and closer to being who he called you to be.

Look at it like this:

1. Do you feel like the Mean Girl in your life is a trial, a challenge?   Yes   No

2. Does she cause you grief?   Yes   No   *Sometimes*

3. Does she wear on your patience?   (Yes)   No

4. Does she test your ability to "turn the other cheek" to your enemy (see Luke 6:29)?   Yes   No

If you answered yes to any of these, let's look deeper into God's Word to find out why she is in your life.

Trials and the Mean Girl:
What Does God Say about It?

(Mean Girl = Trial)

"Consider it pure joy, my ~~brothers~~ [sisters], whenever you face ~~trials~~ [Mean Girls] of many kinds, because you know that ~~the testing of your~~ [a Mean Girl] faith develops perseverance. Perseverance must finish its work so that you may be **mature** and **complete, not lacking anything.**"

Mean Girl translation of James 1:2–4

According to this paraphrased verse, what exactly do Mean Girls do?

_____
_____

What things highlighted in the verse do you want?
all of them
_____

When it comes to all the junk she pulls:

"In this you greatly rejoice, though now [with all kinds of Mean Girls] for a little while you may have had to suffer grief ~~in all kinds of trials~~. These [Mean Girls] have come so that your faith—of greater worth than gold, which perishes even though refined by fire—may be **proved genuine** and may **result in praise, glory and honor** when Jesus Christ is revealed."

1 Peter 1:6–7 MG Version

Why have these Mean Girls come into your life, according to this verse?
So our faith may be proved genuine
_____

How could this be a good thing?
can make our faith stronger
_____

The Mean Girl in your life is not punishment from God. She might not have even been sent by God, but he is still going to use her to purify your faith. Remember, he uses all things together for the good of the people who love him (see Romans 8:28). He uses 'em all—Mean Girls and all—for your good, if you allow it. But if you decide to take this problem and fix it yourself by getting even or mad, then you will waste your chance to prove yourself and pass the test you are going through. Anything you do for selfish ambition or out of anger, hatred, or vengeance is a spiritual failure. You flunk the test. You get an F-. No refining. And when you fail a class, what happens? Yep, repeatsville! You have to take it over again. So you didn't pass the test the first time, and what do you know if *she* doesn't come back again, right at ya. See, if you don't handle trials the way God tells you to—quietly, patiently, lovingly—then you'll start to notice a funny thing: they might just keep repeating till you get them right, whether it's the same girl or a different Mean Girl.

"*Great*," you say. "So I've failed over and over. What am I supposed to do to get it right?" First of all, let me tell you that it's okay that you've failed. Failure just tells you what *not to do*, and that gets you one step closer to what *to* do. And remember, failure is a forgivable offense. There is no condemnation when you are in Christ (see Romans 8:1), only forgiveness, so don't get all dragged down by thinking what a failure you are. That's not coming from God. He wants you to get on with your life and get over it. (If you aren't getting this, stop right now and look up these verses in a Bible: Romans 7:14–8:1; 1 John 1:9.) And remember, you don't have to *feel* forgiven to *be* forgiven. Don't judge your spiritual state based on how you feel, but judge it by what God's Word says. If you don't accept his forgiveness and move on, you are calling him a liar. His Word says you are forgiven (see Acts 10:43; Ephesians 1:7; 1 John 1:9), so you'd best believe his Word.

I hope that now you are starting to see that one of the reasons you have a Mean Girl in your life could be to test your faith and prove it pure. She might be just what you need in order to be purified. But wait, there's more.

DYING TO SELF

Do you believe that God's will and plan is better than yours? Do you believe that what Jesus taught is holy and good for your spirit? If you do, then you will agree that his commands are good and therefore to be followed. So, I ask, how can you prove to him that you believe his words are good unless you have trials in your life to test you? Check it out.

Over 2,000 years ago, Christ died on a cross. He died even though he didn't want to. He begged the Father to find another way (see Mark 14: 36). But when there wasn't another way to take away your sins, he died willingly. And so now, some 2,000 years later, he asks you to die to yourself. That old, sinful, me-protecting self—he asks you to die to that and to live for him. Don't believe me? Then how do you explain these words:

> Then Jesus said to his disciples, "If anyone would come after me, he must deny himself and take up his cross and follow me."
>
> Matthew 16:24

> For you died, and your life is now hidden with Christ in God.
>
> Colossians 3:3

> Those who belong to Christ Jesus have crucified the sinful nature with its passions and desires.
>
> Galatians 5:24

Your Mean Girl might just be your opportunity to die to self. Are you willing to take the challenge and truly die to self?

Before you go any further, consider these words and decide if you believe them. Because if you do, then you have only one choice:

> For it is commendable if a man bears up under the pain of unjust suffering because he is conscious of God. But how is it to your credit if you receive a beating for doing wrong and endure it? But if you suffer for doing good and you endure it, this is commendable before God. To this you were called, because Christ suffered for you, leaving you an example, that you should follow in his steps. "He committed no sin, and no deceit was found in his mouth." When they hurled their insults at him, he did not retaliate; when he suffered, he made no threats. Instead, he entrusted himself to him who judges justly.
>
> 1 Peter 2:19–23

Every believer's goal should be to become more and more like Christ. In this part of God's Word we see that this task means suffering through Mean Girls without retaliation or threats. I know it hurts to have a Mean Girl in your life, but God never asked you to respond to your feelings; he only asks you to obey his Word. His commands never have to do with ordering you to feel good about doing things; they are just commands to do them. So don't ever expect God to command you to *feel* better, but rather expect him to command you to *act* better.

A funny thing happens when you act according to God's Word: you soon find that good feelings follow. If you make it your number one goal to act according to God's commands rather than responding to your Mean Girl's promptings, I promise you that better feelings will soon follow. Yet dying to self isn't an exercise in joy or even peace; it is simply a believer's obedience to a command from their Father. If you live to please God, you will find

that following his commands is the only option for your Mean Girl problem. We'll talk more about the process of dying to self later on, but for now let's keep looking at why she might be in your life.

YOUR CREATION

The final proposal I have for the reason for the existence of your Mean Girl might come as a shock. This one might not apply to you, and if it does, you might not want to believe me. But think about it honestly: sometimes a Mean Girl is your own creation.

A lot of times girls are mean to you because of what you've done, either knowingly or unknowingly. I have had times in my life when I really didn't trust girls. And so I retreated to the world of boys. I spent all my time with them and cut off any contact with girls. As I look back now, I see that it might have made me a few enemies, because what I was showing, subconsciously, was that I didn't like girls. I was passing judgment on them, and who likes to be judged? The way I behaved by avoiding them altogether might have been the very thing that drove them to hate me. So you see, I could have in fact created my own Mean Girls by the way I acted around girls. You might have created your own Mean Girl in other ways. Like maybe you are too sensitive and are always on the defensive when girls talk to you. That makes you a dangerous girl, because they never know when you will blow up, and girls tend to be mean to dangerous girls—it's their faulty self-protection mode.

I hate to even say this, but it might be true, and we have to consider all angles: you might be a Mean Girl yourself, without even knowing it. You've gossiped about someone, hurt their feelings, and now they are after you. You've lied about her and now she's getting you back. Or maybe you just judged her for not being a good girl, so she's after you now. She could be mad at you for any number of reasons, and a lot of them could be something you have done yourself.

So as you read this book, I want you to be totally honest with yourself. If you want to get rid of the Mean Girl in your life, you have to analyze your life. You have to be honest and really assess how you live, what you do, and how you do it. If there are Mean Girls in your life because of something you are doing, then congratulations—that means you have the power to change things. You are actually in a better position than the girl who honestly isn't doing anything to provoke her, because in your case you can do something concrete to change your life today.

Listen, even if a light bulb is going off over your head right now about something you might be doing to make her mad, I want you to understand that changing it today won't make things all better tomorrow. If you've done something mean that has sent her on a rampage, mending fences might take time. But with apologies and forgiveness, over time you *can* fix the mess you've made. So don't start freaking out about this; just keep it in the back of your mind that if your goal is to get rid of your Mean Girl, then you might have to start with yourself. You might not think you have an ounce of mean in you, but I believe that if we are honest, we will all find some bit of mean that can be cleaned up. And with that cleaned up, you might find a world of nice girls open up to you like you've never seen before. So be ready to be honest as you keep reading this book. Be ready to analyze yourself and those girls around you, and by the end you should be ready to take on all the Mean Girls in your life just the way your God wants you to.

I can't tell you why God has allowed this particular Mean Girl in your life. That's something you're going to have to figure out. And you might not find out overnight. But there's one thing I am sure of: the only way to find out is to dig into God's Word, pray, and listen for his answers. The first step to hearing God is reading his Word. In it you will find everything your soul needs to grow and find happiness. So find out all you can about God and his thoughts and commands, and I promise you that your Mean Girl will be less of a problem than ever before. She might not ever change, but you will change, and through that change you will find a hope and peace that surpasses all understanding.

JESUS SPEAKS ON MEAN GIRLS

The best place to start in searching God's Word for truth about mean is in the life and teachings of Jesus. He has a lot to say about mean and a firsthand understanding of the effects of angry and mean people. So let's take a look at Jesus and mean.

Mean Girls aren't a shock to Jesus. They aren't anything new. They existed when he walked the earth, before he walked the earth, and after he left the earth. And I would bet that they will be here long after you leave the earth. Mean Girls exist, and you can't do anything about them without the Word of God in your head and heart. So what does Jesus say about Mean Girls? How does following him make a difference?

The book *Hinds' Feet on High Places* by Hannah Hurnard tells a great story about following Jesus even when it seems ridiculous. In this little book, a young girl named Much Afraid lives her life in fear. When the Shepherd offers to take her away from the land of fearing and up to the high places, she fearfully agrees. During her journey she is tested to her limits, and on one of those occasions her relatives catch up with her and attack her with doubts about the Shepherd who is leading her. As they throw lies at Much Afraid, they tell her that the Shepherd is deceiving her. He is leading her astray, *down* the mountain rather than *up* the mountain. How can that get her to the high places? As she looks around, she sees that it is true. They are going down, not up, and for a moment she starts to think that maybe the Shepherd *is* lying to her. When she asks the Shepherd to explain himself and his apparent deception, he asks her a question: "Would you be willing to trust me . . . even if everything in the wide world seemed to say that I was deceiving you—indeed, that I had deceived you all along?"

What a question. It made me cry as I read it. Would *I* trust him even if everything in the world said he was lying? *Could I do it?* I sobbed. The thought was frightening, but then, just as quickly as Much Afraid, I made my decision. She said,

> "Yes, I'm sure I would, because one thing I know to be true, it is impossible that you should tell a lie. It is impossible that you should deceive me. I know that I am often very frightened at the things which you ask me to do," she added shamefacedly and apologetically, "but I could never doubt you in that way. It's myself I am afraid of, never of you, and though everyone in the world should tell me that you had deceived me, I should know it was impossible."*
>
> *Hannah Hurnard, *Hinds' Feet on High Places*, page 168

What a thing to say. To the world it sounds insane. Incredible. Naive. But to a believer it sounds natural. We follow Christ because we believe him—all of him, all the time. Not just when it makes sense, and not just when it's easy. That's for the half-hearted Christian, the lukewarm one who gets spit out of his mouth (see Revelation 3:16). But for those of us who want to stand the test of time, for those of us who want to rise to new heights and scale new mountains, following him is natural. I've made it my one passion in life to please him, and though I fail over and over again, I know that it is a noble mission. And I know that as part of that mission, I will have to believe and, yes, even do things that might seem the opposite of sane. Some things he's going to ask me to do will be "insane." His command will seem like just plain bad advice to some, but I will follow it anyway. Why? Because of the One who gives it.

If you too want to follow the leading of Christ, if you want to be faithful when your faith is put to the test, then let's start now.

Let's try to figure out how he tells us to treat Mean Girls. Let's dissect his words and see if we can't make them make sense to our feeble little minds.

In Luke 6, after Jesus had just given his disciples and a crowd of people the Beatitudes, he went up to a quieter place to talk to his disciples, and there he told them about Mean Girls. Well, not exactly about Mean *Girls* but about mean people, of which girls are some. In fact, Jesus told them how to treat all people, including people you don't like and people who are your enemies. And this is what he said:

> But if you are willing to listen, I say, love your enemies. Do good to those who hate you. Pray for the happiness of those who curse you. Pray for those who hurt you. If someone slaps you on one cheek, turn the other cheek. If someone demands your coat, offer your shirt also. Give what you have to anyone who asks you for it; and when things are taken away from you, don't try to get them back. Do for others as you would like them to do for you.
>
> Luke 6:27–31 NLT

This is what Jesus is saying in a nutshell:

1. Love girls you don't like. (Love your enemies.)
2. Do good to girls who don't like you. (Do good to those who hate you.)
3. Pray for the girls who slam you. (Pray for the happiness of those who curse you.)
4. Pray for those who are mean to you. (Pray for those who hurt you.)

5. Don't get even. (If someone slaps you on one cheek, turn to him the other also.)
6. Give, give, give till it hurts. (Give what you have to anyone who asks you for it; and when things are taken away from you, don't try to get them back.)
7. Treat others like you want to be treated. (Do for others as you would like them to do for you.)

Jesus is talking about his kind of love here: unconditional and not a feeling but an action. That's the kind of love we all want—to be loved by someone no matter what you do wrong, or how much you hurt them, or how they might feel at the time. It's the love that God has for his children. It's not about what they do wrong or right. No, it's just about the fact that they have been adopted as daughters of the Father, and that's that, period. So Jesus was teaching his disciples to love like the Father does. Unconditionally. Now, that seems really romantic when you are talking about your true love. Of course you want him to love you unconditionally. You even want your parents to do that. It's a beautiful thing when you receive it—but did you know that he also wants *you* to give your *enemies* the same kind of love?

It's a weak faith that only loves the one who loves them back. I always say that if you want to know the true character of a person, then watch how they treat people who can do nothing for them—or better yet, watch how they treat their enemies. As you watch their behavior, you will see who they really are, because when the rubber hits the road, that's when the true you comes out. And that's why Jesus says that we are supposed to love our enemies like this. He wants your true character, that same character he has, to be seen in you.

If you want to know the **true character** of a **person**, then watch how they treat people who can do nothing for them—or better yet, watch how they treat their enemies. That will show you their true character.

So if Jesus is giving us a blueprint for our character, let's look to see how it applies to our lives. Right here in your book, write down the names of the girls at school or at work who are mean. Write down at least one girl who is hurting you or trying to control you.

_____

_____

_____

_____

_____

_____

_____

Now take a look at the list below, and this time put their names in the blanks. This is your to-do list from God. This is how you are to handle the Mean Girl.

1. Love _____

2. Do good to _____

3. Pray for _____

4. Pray for _____

5. Don't get even with _____

6. Give, give, give to _____
   till it hurts.

7. Treat _____ like I want to
   be treated.

Now take a look at this list. Can you imagine doing all those things? Does it seem possible for you to agree with God's Word when it comes to loving the Mean Girl? Love is obviously the command, but how in the world do you do it when you don't feel any love for her whatsoever? To answer that, let me ask you this: if love were a feeling, then could it be commanded? For example, could someone command you to feel frustrated? Or happy? Or sad, even? Let me answer that for you: no. Feelings can't be commanded, so since the Bible commands us to love, love can't be a feeling. When God commands us to love, he wants us to take action in spite of what we are feeling. If you think about it, this makes total sense. If God wanted you to wait till you *felt* love, then love would become all about you. It would be a self-centered kind of thing, like "I will only love you if you make me feel good." But that's where the world gets it wrong. Love isn't about how you feel. We aren't called to love to get something out of it; we are called to love so someone else gets something out of it.

LOVE = GIVING

So what is love if it isn't a feeling? Another stellar question. In order to understand love, let's look at love himself and see how he operates. Of course I am talking about God, for "God is love" (1 John 4:8).

> For **God so loved the world** that he gave his one and only Son, that whoever believes in him shall not perish but have eternal life.
>
> John 3:16

> I live by faith in the **Son of God,** who **loved me** and gave himself for me.
>
> Galatians 2:20

Do you see the pattern? God loved, so God gave. Love is first born in giving. Giving is about caring for the other person and what they need for faith and life. "God so loved the world." Notice it doesn't say, "The world made God feel so good that he loved it." Again, not to beat a dead pony, but love isn't about feeling good. God set an example for us in his love. And the life of Christ that we as believers seek to imitate is a clear example of love. Do you really think that Christ was overcome with love and joy as he was being whipped and nailed to a cross? Love is about giving, not getting. Love is about caring, not being cared for. Love is about helping, not being helped. Love reaches outside itself and gives to others. Love isn't concerned with self; it is concerned with others. The love that God commands is pure, holy, and untainted by self-gratification.

A girl once asked me, "Isn't it hypocritical to do nice things for people when you don't feel like it, when you don't even like them?" According to the world, yes, but hypocrisy isn't about feelings any more than love is. You don't judge a hypocrite based on whether they felt like doing what they did or not; you judge based on whether they did what they believed or not. *Doing what God calls you to do is never hypocrisy, even when you don't feel like it.* A hypocrite is a person who doesn't do what God calls them to do when they believe that his commands are good and true and should be followed. Or when someone tells others that trusting God is good but fails to do it themselves—that is being a hypocrite. Let's face it, we are called to do what God commands whether we like it or not, and love is no different. You do it because he tells you to. Feelings are off the table.

It's like this: Every day I get up and go to work (even though I work from home). Some days I don't feel like getting out of bed, let alone getting dressed and opening up my email, but I do it anyway. Does that make me a hypocrite? No, doing what you have to do even when you don't feel like it is never hypocrisy. It's called *integrity*. So it won't make you a hypocrite to give love when you don't feel loving.

MEAN GIRL LOVE

What I want you to understand from all this is that you don't give love in order to get what you want. Ever. That's where hypocrisy lies. Love isn't about getting something out of it. Not even with the Mean Girl. Even though it's true that if you obey God and love the Mean Girl, you might find that you've won her over or at least stopped her attacks, your obedience to God should never be for selfish reasons. Don't follow him to get things. And don't obey his command to love in order to get something in return. Your goal in loving the Mean Girl is not to get her to change. Your goal is to honor God by loving your enemies. A wonderful side effect of obeying God might just be that she stops picking on you, but that isn't your concern when you are loving God's way. Whether or not she changes is in his hands, and it can't be your main goal. It is simply a by-product of faith.

"I do not like to think of you as needing to have 'things' pleasant around you when you have God within you. Surely He is enough to content any soul. If He is not enough here, how will it be in the future life when we have only Him Himself?"

—Hannah Whitall Smith

GOSSIP GIRLS, REVENGERS, AND OTHER MEAN GIRLS

Gossip girls, revenge seekers, liars—there are all kinds of mean. And each one has its own problems. In the list of Mean Girl weapons you will probably find one that fits your particular problem. Check out why she does what she does and what you can do in response to her in order to keep the faith. The way you react will determine her next attack, so be very careful, and you might be able to get away from your Mean Girl unscathed.

THE GOSSIP GIRL

For Mean Girls, gossip can be the currency that buys them a place in another girl's heart. It's a twisted bonding ritual for the MG. You know the feeling. When you tell a friend something you heard or saw and you know you shouldn't be repeating it, you feel the endorphins running through your blood, almost giving you a little buzz. It's a great feeling, and you become dark soul sisters. *"What dainty morsels rumors are—but they sink deep into one's heart"* (Proverbs 18:8 NLT). Gossip, ah, how invigorating! And you know that as soon as the popular girl wants to dish you some big G, then you're in. Gossip is your express pass into the in crowd. Without gossip, a lot of girls wouldn't have anything to talk about.

The truth is, a lot of us gossip, but we don't really do it to be mean; we just do it because, well, it's harder to control our curiosity and tongue than to play the gossip game. And with some friends, it's almost like a requirement or expectation that you've gotta dish. You wanna be friends? Then you gotta share juicy G. But gossip is more than just a "fun" way to bond with a best friend; it's a sin in the face of God (see Leviticus 19:16). And not only is it a sin, but it's a sin that deeply hurts the subject of your gossip party. In

Common sense indicates that 99.99% of girls not focused on God gossip.

fact, it can totally destroy the object of its attention. And Mean Girls know that. They use gossip like it's a machine gun, mowing down every girl they have it in for. And if there isn't anything true to talk about, they'll make something up.

> A gossip tells secrets, so don't hang around with someone who talks too much.
>
> —King Solomon (Proverbs 20:19 NLT)

When a girl gossips, it doesn't have to be the truth. It just has to sound good and juicy. The thing to remember is that the gossip isn't only about you; it's also about her bonding with her friends, as sick as that is. You might not be able to keep it from hurting, but you can keep it from destroying you. And here's how:

1. Ignore her. Don't give her any reaction. Ignore her words. See, her goal is to make you mad. When she reaches her goal, it's like she gets extra lives on her video game, and she just keeps coming back for more battles. Always keep in mind the goal of the game: the Mean Girl wants to hurt you, and she knows she has hurt you when she gets a reaction. We can find the wisdom behind this truth in an ancient proverb written by King Solomon which goes something like this: "*A fool shows her annoyance at once, but a smart girl overlooks an insult*" (Proverbs 12:16, *Mean Girls* paraphrase). It's an ancient truth: ignore the gossip and you prove your wisdom. Unfortunately, some really Mean Girls will never lose interest in hurting you, no matter how cool you act. But you can't let that change your allegiance to God's Word.

Okay, so how do you ignore her evil ways? Glad you asked. Ignoring gossip has more to do with acting like you've ignored it than really ignoring it. When you hear about the rumor, don't get upset, at least not in public, and definitely not in front of her! I repeat, *don't get upset.* Don't yell at your friend, "But that just isn't true!" or storm up to the gossiper and give her a piece of your mind. That is not ignoring it. That is playing right into her game. Mean Girls love to see you squirm; it's why they do what they do. So never let 'em see you squirm.

2. Prove her wrong. The second thing you can do when a Gossip Girl strikes is to prove her wrong with your actions. Think about a well-respected newspaper versus a supermarket tabloid. One thoroughly researches a story and worries about getting the facts right. The other only worries about selling copies and knows that stretching the truth (or even making things up) is going to sell enough copies to pay all the lawsuits their lies or half-truths bring. The thing is, you and I already know that supermarket tabloids can rarely be believed. So people that really know you or take the time to get to know you are going to know her lies aren't true (or at least suspect it). But for those who don't really know you, you can prove the Gossip Girl wrong by making sure your actions don't match the gossip when you're around others, especially those listening to the gossip. Because when the Gossip Girl says stuff about you that isn't true and her friends start seeing in your actions that the gossip is all a bunch of lies, the Gossip Girl loses points in this sick game of mean.

Now, if you *did* do the deeds that the Gossip Girl is spreading, then I'm sorry that someone so mean is exposing your mistakes or flaws for her enjoyment and your suffering. But you can still prove her wrong with your actions going forward. You'll basically be making the statement that, yes, you made a mistake, but that's not a part of your permanent character. Even a supermarket tabloid gets a story right once in a while, and sometimes that exposure is just the kick in the pants that a celebrity needs to get their act

together. If a Gossip Girl gets something right in her twisted reporting, you can actually turn the tables on her and thank her for exposing something in your life you should've handled better. And if you change those things in your life and the Gossip Girl keeps churning out the same gossip, in the end she just looks like one of those supermarket tabloids—she'll always have an audience who wants to hear the latest lie, but you've proven that she's just a trashy tabloid that no one takes seriously. (The Bible agrees: see 1 Peter 2:12; Proverbs 19:11; Proverbs 20:3.)

So to win the gossip game, ignore the Gossip Girl and prove her wrong with your actions. Game, set, match: you win. Play the game right, and your gossip nightmare may just disappear.

A man's wisdom gives him patience;

it is to his glory to overlook an offense.

—King Solomon (Proverbs 19:11)

THE NAME-CALLER

It's weird, but have you ever noticed how it can make you feel so much better just to call someone a name when they've ticked you off? I think we're all tempted to do it once in a while. It's human nature. So what do you do when the Mean Girl nails you with her name-calling? How do you handle the hurt of being labeled, outed, or smeared by a name-caller?

1. Don't let her see you sweat. Just like other Mean Girl tactics, name-calling is used to hurt you and make you mad. So the number one thing you have to remember is, *don't let her see you sweat.* Don't react emotionally in any way. When you get hurt and retaliate, she wins, plain and simple. So hold your tongue unless you have something nice or funny to say. For example, I knew a girl who had really bad buckteeth that didn't even fit in her mouth. One time a girl called her a vampire and then looked at her friends and giggled. The bucktoothed girl looked at them, smiled, and said, "I know, check this out," and she lifted her upper lip and made a face like a rabbit. Everyone laughed. The girls just didn't expect it. It totally caught them off guard. They had slammed her, but she totally didn't mind; in fact, she showed them she wasn't an emotional weakling and that she was probably more confident than any of them.

2. Don't make yourself a victim. Unfortunately, sometimes name-calling can turn into labeling. You might be called a geek, and then it just sticks. Again, don't sweat your pocket protector. Take it in stride. Remember, Microsoft guru Bill Gates is a geek, and he's one of the richest and most famous men in the world. Don't let the label others put on you ruin who you are or who you become. If it's true, then own it. Change it into something positive. And if it's not true, then start the anti-label campaign. Prove them wrong with your actions by being who you *really* are, not who they are trying to make you.

Don't allow someone to make you a victim of their tongue.* If you do, you're surrendering control to them to be a force of negative change in your life. Remember, no matter what people call you, they can't change who you are. Only you and Christ can do that. If you choose to let others make you into their image, you lose—and you deny Christ, because he calls you to be made into his image, to *"put on the new self, which is being renewed in knowledge **in the image of its Creator**"* (Colossians 3:10). Christ died to set you free—free from the enemy controlling you, free from your negative self, and, of course, free from the Mean Girl. You might not be feeling it right now, but it's true: you are the child of a king, not the punch line of a bad joke. If you want to know how to turn it around and be the girl you were made to be, find out what pleases your Father. Find out how he wants you to act and react.

You live in a hurting world, one that has a ton of girls in it who hurt so bad that the only way they see to ease their pain is to put *others* in more pain. But you aren't like that. Your pain has hope. Your pain has release. When you get tired of being the butt of their jokes, remember this: *"Blessed is the man who perseveres under trial, because when he has stood the test, he will receive the crown of life that God has promised to those who love him"* (James 1:12).

> But he said to me, "My grace is sufficient for you, for my power is made perfect in weakness." Therefore I will boast all the more gladly about my weaknesses, so that Christ's power may rest on me. That is why, for Christ's sake, I delight in weaknesses, in insults, in hardships, in persecutions, in difficulties. For when I am weak, then I am strong.
>
> —2 Corinthians 12:9–10

THE REVENGERS

If you are a girl and you live on this planet, you have probably had another girl try to get revenge on you. You did something either accidentally or on purpose that she didn't like, and she went after you. Revenge seems to be as essential to the female as shoes. Most girls operate by the saying, "Don't get mad, get even." After all, some people think that if there is no God and no one who is looking out for you and protecting you, then you have to take control yourself. But we are different. With a belief in God, we don't have to get revenge, because it isn't our gig, it's God's. And what a relief. Trouble is that most girls don't get this, so they are going to forever be after other girls to get revenge.

Before we go any further, if you really did do something that hurt the Revenger, you've got to apologize. Your motivation shouldn't be to stop the revenge (though that may be the result) but to do what's right because you really should apologize. You don't like it when someone hurts you, so loving your neighbor like yourself means saying you're sorry.

Now, even if you didn't do what she thinks you did, there are only a few ways to stop the revenge cycle. You can't stop her from attacking you, but you don't have to fight back the same way. Here are three keys to ending the nasty cycle of revenge:

1. Don't retaliate. You don't need to get revenge for her revenge. Her anger is hers; don't let her infect you with it. Remember, she's the one suffering because she's the one who hurts so badly that she feels a need to hurt you back. You don't have to feel that way because you know that God works all things together for the good of those who love him (see Romans 8:28). So don't say anything mean back, and don't do anything to get revenge. Just laugh it off, or at least hide your hurt until you're alone. You'll kill the revenge cycle right there. If you don't take my advice and do decide to get revenge, then all bets are off, and the war is on. Getting revenge only makes things worse and makes you meaner, so lay off!

2. Don't tell. If you run off and tell a teacher or someone in authority, you run the risk of keeping the revenge cycle going. Your Mean Girl will think she has to get you back for telling, and the cycle keeps on spinning. So if she hasn't threatened your life or your security at school or work and hasn't hurt you physically, try to lay low.

3. Pray. This might sound totally trite because you've heard it so much, but you need to learn it now. Pray for her. God calls us to pray for our enemies (see Matthew 5:44). This does two things: It gets our minds off of ourselves, and it gets God on the case.

THE 3-WAY CALLER

The infamous 3-way call or IM chat. Have you ever had it done to you? Your friend calls you and nonchalantly asks you about another friend or a guy. And after you've spilled your guts, you hear another person on the line who was listening in the entire time. Argh! Horrible for you. But for the other two it's juicy—the best way to find out what someone *really* thinks. Trouble is, it's an invasion of privacy and a way to royally mess up your relationships. And don't forget, if someone will do something for you, they'll do it to you. In other words, if someone will 3-way call *for you,* they'll 3-way call *on you* just as fast.

Mean Girls dig the 3-way call because it's a power trip. They can gather much-needed information *and* embarrass you to death, and all in a matter of five minutes.

Your best defense against a 3-way call?

1. Shut up. Don't ever, and I mean *ever,* say anything about anyone that you wouldn't want them to hear you say. Yes, 3-way calling, as terrible as it is, might actually be a way to get you to start talking the way God would have you talk. You've heard the saying, "If you don't have anything good to say, then don't say anything at all." It's a cliché for a reason—it's true. So shut up. If you want to avoid 3-way call trauma, then never, I mean *never,* say anything mean about anyone, to anyone. Then they can't trick you on a 3-way, and they will never be able to get you with their meanness.

2. Don't do it. Don't go whining about girls 3-way calling if you are doing the same thing to other girls! Remember, you are going to be judged for the same thing you are getting all sassy about—or haven't you heard? *"Stop judging others, and you will not be judged. For others will treat you as you treat them. Whatever measure you use in judging others, it will be used to measure how you are judged"* (Matthew 7:1–2 NLT).

So don't do it. Never, ever 3-way call someone in secret! It's just not cool. What it really says is that you are so completely wrapped up in what someone thinks of you that you have to find out if whatever it is *you* think *they* think is true. Bad, bad, bad. Remember that God's really not too keen on you seeking to get the approval of other people over him (see Galatians 1:10).

SLAMMERS AND OTHER HATERS

A lot of girls aren't content to hate you themselves—they want everyone else to hate you too, or at least to say they do. Slam books or other cruel stuff they might write in their blog and the like are evil and angry attempts to rise above you by bringing you down way low. Mean Girls want to make you mad, and who wouldn't be mad if the entire class signed a notebook or website saying they hated you? It's cruel and unusual punishment. If you are the victim of a slam campaign, then you are the victim of a Really Mean Girl.

What do you do?

1. Use evil for good. This slam is probably the worst thing another girl could do to you, and she has no right. But I can't give you a magical way to get through it. The only thing you can do is use her evil as a chance for you to hold on tight to God. He promises that if you do, you will see the other side. Jesus said, "I have told you these things, so that in me you may have peace. In this world you will have trouble. But take heart! I have overcome the world" (John 16:33). You are always on God's mind, even in the midst of this. Ask yourself, *Where is my hope? What is God doing in this? How can I use this trial to draw closer to him?* You can draw closer by relying on him to use stuff like this to make you more holy, by reading more of the Bible, and by praying more. Some of the most amazing spiritual experiences and advances in my life have come from terrible grief. Will this horrible thing done to you be used for good?

> In this you greatly rejoice, though now for a little while you may have had to suffer grief in all kinds of trials. These have come so that your faith—of greater worth than gold, which perishes even though refined by fire—may be proved genuine and may result in praise, glory and honor when Jesus Christ is revealed.
>
> 1 Peter 1:6–7

2. Don't get mad. The Mean Girl's goal is to make you mad, so when you react in anger, she wins. So what if you don't react in anger? How many points does she get? Zero!

3. Don't get sad. Another point for her is when she makes you sad. And if you cry, that's major pointage to her side. And if you react in the opposite way as what the slam book says—for example, if it says you are a mean witch but you react by being nice and kind to everyone—you actually get points. So think about this like a game or a battle. You have to think of it logically and not emotionally, or you will lose. And the more you lose, the more she comes after you, because she's lazy and she loves an easy win.

4. Ignore 'em. Do all you can to ignore her, even if it means holding on with all you've got till you get home and you can vent. Be careful with this one though; mean people hate to be ignored. They hate it when their precious attack goes unnoticed. If you find this just increases her intensity, look to use humor or caring responses instead, or maybe even option five, which is . . .

5. Confront carefully. Ignoring is usually best, but if you feel sure that God is telling you to confront the girl, never do it

in front of her friends. (See "Standing Up to Your Mean Girl," page 143.) She will be trying to impress them, and you'll never get through to her. And don't do it on the phone or on IM, because you don't know who she might be with. Find a place where you can be alone, like the library or her house. Before you say anything, spend time figuring out how to say it in love. You have every right to speak for yourself; just be sure you speak in love and peace and don't corner her. You might try to ask her what you have done to make her hate you. When she tells you, don't argue with her. Remember, this isn't about you feeling better but about reaching out to another girl in love.

6. Know when to tell. You have to judge the degree of mean to decide what you should do about it. If the slam book or blog or whatever it is starts threatening violence, then you have to tell someone in authority. But if it's not something that scares you, then don't tell, because telling unnecessarily will only add fuel to her fire and keep the cycle going. Remember, when Mean Girls get bored, they often give up. Talk about this concept with your parents so they understand and support where you're coming from. If you're not entertainment for your Mean Girl, she will eventually get tired of bothering you.

Unfortunately, as I've said before, some girls might never give up. You might have to put up with her hatred as long as you are in the same school together. Just don't let her evil become your evil. Stay strong and trust God with your Mean Girl.

"It is God's business, not ours, to care for what we have. God is able to protect what we possess. We can trust him [with our things and our relationships]. The lock on the door is not what protects the house. Simplicity means the freedom to trust God for these and all things."

—Richard Foster, *Celebration of Discipline*

CYBERSPACERS

Some Mean Girls are too wimpy to attack you in person, so they resort to cyberspace.* Maybe you've gotten a nasty text on your cell or an IM that insulted your clothes or your body. In some freaky cases embarrassing pictures or videos are circulating. What would you do if you were this real-life kid? A 15-year-old (who shall remain nameless) videotaped himself acting out a scene from *Star Wars* with a golf ball retriever as his light saber. Soon some other kids got ahold of the video, doctored it up with music from *The Matrix*, and put it on YouTube. Soon this kid was one of the most downloaded guys of the year. Utter embarrassment! What would you do if something like that happened to you? Would you drop out of school? Go loopy on us? How would you handle it? How would God have you handle it? Check out these two scenarios and decide which one you think is victorious and faithful:

Option 1. You freak out so much you change schools so you don't have to be seen again by anyone who saw you on video. But the next school you go to has seen you already too. It's all

*1 in 17 kids ages 10 to 17 had been threatened or harassed online.

over the Internet. So you drop out again, and your mom home-schools you while you go to a counselor to ease the pain. Now you're all alone and the laughingstock of your city, maybe even the world. Did you win?

Option 2. You go to school and ask the teacher if you can talk to the class. She says yes, and you give the best Oscar accep-tance speech anyone could ever give. You show a clip of your video and point out all the subtleties of your geekiness. The class goes crazy with laughter as you smile and say, "Thanks for mak-ing me the most downloaded girl in America! And thanks to the Academy!"

Instantly you're the funniest girl in school. Everyone loves funny people, and you just took an embarrassment and made it a joke. Remember, if you make fun of yourself, you take away the power of the slam from the other person. In the movie *8 Mile* (rated R, btw) Rabbit, the character played by rapper Eminem, is in a freestyle rapping contest where the goal is to slam another contestant in front of the roaring crowd. When Rabbit's life hits its most humiliating depths, he is sure to lose. But knowing his com-petitor will make fun of his failures and embarrassments, Rabbit turns the tables and rhymes with all his might about his miserable life. He points out all the bad things that have happened to him. He mocks himself and makes jokes, and by the end of his rap, his opponent, who has to go second, has nothing left to make fun of because Rabbit did it all himself. If you feel this desperate, then you might want to consider throwing in the towel and joining the crowd. If you can make it a joke that you are in on and own, you can use a humiliating moment as an upper instead of a downer. It's called "stealing their thunder."

Unlike Rabbit's situation, it's physically impossible for you to go nose to nose with your Mean Girl in cyberspace (or in an underground rap contest). So what do you do? If you want to avoid, get away from, or "Rabbitize" cyber-attacks, here are some things to consider:

1. Ignore them. When you are on the Internet, act the same as in person. Ignore them. Don't argue back with the Mean Girl. Just hit delete or close. If you get an email from someone you don't know or trust, don't read it. Just delete it.

2. Get off the Internet. If you know a Mean Girl has a blog, what are you doing going to her site to read it? If you're getting cyber-slammed, take a break and unplug. Start to spend less time on the Internet and more time with friends and family. Read a book; play with the dog or your kid brother. The more time you spend glued to the Net, the more chances for cyber-attack.

3. Beware. You never know if the person IMing or emailing you is really who they say they are. It could be someone pretending to be someone else. And don't believe everything you read or see on the Internet. If you are naïve, you can be taken for a ride. Be smart. I'll say it again: don't trust everything you read (except this book, of course).

4. Hang up the phone. I know it seems impossible, but turn your cell off. Don't have it on all day for text messaging. If you aren't available for harassing, then they are less likely to harass you.

5. Laugh. Remember not to take yourself too seriously. If people are circulating photos or videos of you, remember to laugh with them. See if their blog or website allows you to post comments. Be funny and pull a "Rabbit" out of your hat by posting an even crazier picture of yourself. If you or someone you know has the skills, make your own blog and get creative. Lighten up. When you take yourself and them too seriously, you make a bigger mess of a little thing that you might not even remember ten years from now.

THE VIOLENT GIRL

Some girls are not only mean but also violent. They are so enraged by the actions or even the appearance of others that they lash out in violence, just hoping to feel better about themselves and prove others are worse than people think. While violence is so much worse than the things we've been talking about, it's part of the same problem, except gone really, really bad. The truth is, girls who want to physically fight other girls are in a world of pain. If violence is the first, second, or third option for a girl, then something inside her is terribly wrong. She is blaming the world for her pain and hoping that violence will somehow soothe her. She's basically a Really Mean Girl out of control. And so she requires a whole new set of rules. What we've been talking about so far is doing things to avoid getting to this level of mean. But if you are afraid of violence from other girls or have been threatened in any way, then something has to be done.

Here are some early warning signs of these girls in extreme pain. If you know a girl like this and she just so happens to be your Mean Girl, then you'll need to do some things to protect yourself from her potential violent outbreaks. If you notice any of the following in your Mean Girl, you could be dealing with a Violent Girl who might get physical with you:

- loss of temper on a regular basis
- any history of physical fighting
- significant vandalism or property damage
- uses drugs or alcohol

- prefers risk-taking activities
- detailed plans to commit acts of violence
- announcing threats or plans for hurting others
- enjoys hurting animals
- carrying a weapon*

* Adapted from *Safeguarding Our Children: An Action Guide*, U.S. Departments of Education and Justice, http://www.ed.gov/admins/lead/safety/actguide/action_guide.pdf

If you are afraid of your Mean Girl or have been hurt physically by her, then it's time to get some help. Here are some things you should do if you are scared of another girl:

Never be alone with her.

Avoid her as much as possible.

Remove whatever it is that is making her mad (i.e., don't talk about her, gossip about her, or crush on her boyfriend).

Don't be proud. Let her be right on the little things if it will stop her fighting.

Don't argue with her. (You can never win an argument with a crazy person, so don't try—it will only make her mad.)

Tell someone you trust: teacher, principal, counselor, pastor, parent, or police.

Find someone in authority who will protect you by walking with you to your car, etc.

Check to see if your school has an anonymous school violence hotline and use it if you need to turn someone in for professed or suspected violence against you or anyone else.

Don't be predictable. Vary your routines so they can't prepare for an attack.

If you get a physical threat in any way—email, voicemail, text, face-to-face—report it to the police. It's harassment and considered a criminal offense.

Always stay where there are plenty of people. Never go to the bathroom alone.

Get involved in healthy activities like sports and clubs that keep you busy and with lots of people.

The last thing you want to do is give a Violent Girl a reason to hurt you. So use the techniques we've talked about so far to avoid making matters worse. Remember in all things that dying to self and not having to have the last word will not only make your spiritual life better but will make life with the Mean Girl better as well. If there was ever a time to shut up (to her face) and not show your anger or pain, it's with a Violent Girl. The cycle of mean started with her will only escalate into something you don't want. So avoid confrontations with the Violent Girl at all costs and be ready to communicate any escalation to the authority figures in your life.

One final tactic for dealing with the Violent Girl is prayer. You'll need God's hand when it comes to the Violent Girl—more than anything else at this point. Pray for her soul, her mind, and her heart. Pray that she will find a way out of her need for violence. The Violent Girl is a tragically sick girl, and she needs the touch of Christ's hand as much as anyone else.

These are just a few mean girls and their tactics. No matter what her weapon of choice, a Mean Girl is a hard thing to live with, but if you trust and follow these tips you might just find that they'll start to lose their power over your life. No matter what the outcome, keep your eyes looking upward and remember that he uses all things together for the good of those who love him (Romans 8:28).

WHO'S THE FATTEST?

Girls compete with each other about who is fattest. You know it's true—heck, you've done it. "I'm so fat today," your friend says. And to ease her troubled mind, you say, "Well, at least you aren't as fat as me!" Or a girl says, "I hate it, you are so skinny!" and you say, "Oh, no, I'm totally bloated." You grasp at anything you can to point out that you indeed are not skinny but fat. How sweet of you, and oh how self-degrading. But let me ask: why do you think that being the fattest makes you better or her feel great? Why do we as girls think that to be skinny is an insult to the other girl, so much so that we have to quickly deny any connection whatsoever to skinny?

It's a strange phenomenon that I've noticed in my journey, this condition peculiar to girls—you just don't hear guys arguing over who's fattest. Somehow cutting yourself down is the only acceptable response to a compliment in girl world. It's as if a compliment is a hot potato or a flaming arrow that has to be dodged and denied. And it isn't just about weight. Remember a girl telling you, "I love that outfit," and your response of "Oh, this old thing? It's all I could find to put on today, and I feel totally hideous." Or try saying, "I'm really bad at math," and watch another girl say something like "At least you're better at it than me." It's always the same. Deflect the compliment by slamming yourself.

In girl world the compliment can be an interesting knife of dissection. And it serves as a precision cutting instrument in the hands of a conniving girl. In our discussion of why girls are mean, the compliment phenomenon is a very useful occurrence to understand.

When you get a compliment from a girl, your immediate response is probably to deny it. That's because you assume that now that she's pointed out a good thing about you, she must be feeling inferior. So you choose to degrade yourself by denying the compliment to save her from feeling any worse about herself and to avoid getting targeted as one to be knocked down because you've got it together. Add on something that cuts yourself down, and *bam*! You've just gifted the giver with a beautiful package of your own.

This seems to be a natural female response designed both to protect the feelings of others and to keep them from hating you. We are born to care for others, not to destroy them, so our natural response to a potential hurt feeling is to scramble to the rescue. Many a researcher might say that girls tend to deny compliments and turn them to self-degradation because of low self-esteem. And to that I say, phooey. There might be a smidge of bad body image in the degradation, but for the most part it's self-protection. I believe that when you deny a compliment, your main goal is to protect the feelings of the giver and thus save yourself from creating another enemy. In other words, the girl has thrown out an insecurity, something that she's potentially jealous of, and your job is to make her feel secure again. So when you deny a compliment, your main goal is to protect the feelings of the giver and thus save yourself from creating another enemy.

The trouble is that your mind is simple. It believes whatever it reads, sees, or hears the most, especially from you. You're the expert on you, aren't you? And so if you continue to tell others your faults in order to make them feel good about themselves, you continue to reinforce in your mind a negative self-image. And *that's* when the research proves true. It's a self-fulfilling prophecy. Imagine if I were to tell myself every morning as I lay in bed,

> *I hate mornings.*
> *I hate getting up.*
> *I'm not a morning person.*
> *I just hate mornings.*

I would find it very, very hard to get up. Why? Well, maybe it's true that I'm more of a night person, but the truth is that I've just made it worse by training my brain to think that it not only loves the nights but *hates* the mornings. But I could choose to stop this negative input and replace it with something more positive and true, like,

> *I can get a lot of stuff done in the mornings.*
> *I have the ability to get up early.*
> *Getting up early isn't as hard as I thought.*

Then I would find that getting up can get easier. Scripture backs this up in the book of Proverbs where it tells us that "as he thinketh in his heart, so is he." Your actions are the result of your thoughts. Think tired thoughts and you'll be tired.

God created us so that thinking good, honest, and godly thoughts brings us peace. Researchers even found the power of this positive thinking when they studied athletes. They gave the same workout routine to two groups of bicyclists. They all had to ride five miles a day around the city. Half of that time they spent riding up hills and the other half down hills. One group was taken aside and told that they were to think for at least ten minutes a day about how much they hate riding up hills. The other group was told that they were to tell themselves for at least ten minutes a day what a great workout they were going to get riding up hills. At the end of a week, they compared the two groups' riding times. The first group, those who told themselves that they hated hills, had considerably worse times than the other group. They said that when they got to the hills, they just lost energy. Their minds learned what they told them and acted upon it.

Your mind is listening to everything you tell it. So be careful about what you say, or you will create a monster. Tell yourself every day that you are fat and watch your mind try to make sure that's true. Your mind tends to think it's right. If it hears that you are fat over and over, then it becomes convinced that you are fat regardless of the real truth. That's why girls with eating disorders see themselves as fat when we all see them as thin. The mind believes what we repeatedly think and say. Think about what you want your mind to do and to create. Think about it very carefully next time you want to respond to a compliment in a self-degrading way. Is that really who you want to make yourself to be? If not, then zip it! Don't say anything but thank you.

So how do you deal with compliments in a world of girls? Take a look at the different uses of the fake compliment and learn the best way to avoid giving them and getting them.

THE COMPLIMENT WITH A TWIST

"You are so skinny, I hate you." Is it a compliment? Is it a slam? This one, delivered with just the right sweet tone, is a slam in compliment's clothing. How could anyone get mad after receiving a compliment? So what if there is an angry message attached to it? You can't deny that the compliment was there, so you immediately look for a way to degrade yourself to make the giver of this double-edged compliment feel better. What a great delivery of

an evil cut—she makes you feel bad for her after she has slammed you. It's ingenious, really.

So what do you do with this combo? How do you react? Just like you do with every other slam: smile and move along. A lot of girls might not realize that this combo can be hurtful, so give them the benefit of the doubt and trust that they mean well. But as you practice controlling your own mean streak, stay away from the compliment/slam combo. If you want to compliment someone, don't tack on a hateful comment. It isn't necessary or complimentary. Remember, girls are afraid of ticking other girls off, so don't give them cause to fear. It just isn't cool!

THE HIDDEN SLAM

"I love that dress." Sounds simple enough, but we all know that it's not *what you say* but *how you say it* and what you really mean that counts. Either way, with the hidden slam compliment, you have to take it with a smile. If you fight back or act snotty in return, you lose. I repeat: you lose. She gets a point by making you mad. So even though the compliment she just threw at you wasn't meant as a compliment, just smile sweetly and move along. Heck, you might even throw in a "thank you" and a smile. Do all you can to take it as a compliment and move on.

If it is totally obvious that she is being mean and doesn't have an ounce of sincerity—i.e., if she is with a group of girls and they all giggle as she says it—you can *still* just smile knowingly and keep on moving. There's no use saying anything mean in return. It will only make matters worse. Her presence is merely a blip on the radar screen, nothing more. She shouldn't rock your world or impact it in any way, so don't let her. Don't make it more than what it is: a catty little comment. In ten years it won't mean a thing. (Besides, you don't always know people's intentions. She might actually be trying to be nice, so always react gracefully and you always win. You never want to get framed as a Mean Girl by attacking a compliment. Bad move.)

And if you are a big fan of the hidden slam, shame on you. Your job in life is not to destroy people but to build them up. If you are bent on destroying others, know that God is watching and he isn't pleased. So avoid the hidden slam. It doesn't do anybody any good, and it isn't funny.

HANDLING A COMPLIMENT SO THAT EVERYONE WINS

The best way to handle a compliment is to accept it and give it back. Simply say thank you and then give a compliment back. Warning: girls are often afraid of a confident girl, so be prepared—when you say thank you, they might be shocked, but complimenting them back will soothe their shock a bit. It's hard being a confident girl. It can leave you open as a target because the Mean Girl will feel insecure with you around. But stand your ground. Just because she is defective doesn't mean you have to be as well.

FROM THE OUTSIDER TO THE SHY GIRL: GIRLS THEY LOVE TO HATE

No one has any right to hate you, but not having a right never stopped anybody. For centuries girls have hated other girls and girls have asked "Why?" In the pages that follow, you will find out some of the warped reasons why your Mean Girl might hate you.

Your main goal is to get the Mean Girl to leave you alone. When you understand more about her, you might be able to find ways to distract her or even motivate her to change herself. This section is all about the kinds of girls Mean Girls love to hate and what you can do if you are one of these girls.

THE OUTSIDER

While speaking to a group of girls at a school, I was told the story of a girl who started going to the school and soon trans-ferred. The girl who told the story smiled from the front row as she said, "This girl was just weird. No one could figure her out. I mean, we tried to be nice to her, but she just wasn't nice back. So one day we took her wallet from her and flushed it down the toilet. It was pretty funny. Then we just yelled at her whenever we saw her, 'Why won't you talk, freak girl?' And before you know it, she had to transfer to another school. She just couldn't handle the pressure." The storyteller looked around the room at all her friends and enemies and smiled triumphantly.

Our topic was Mean Girls, and she felt like that was the perfect story to tell us about Mean Girls—the Mean Girl being the one who had to transfer. "Why was she mean?" I asked. "Because she wouldn't talk to any of us," she said quickly, as if I were completely clueless. "We're glad she's gone," she added.

In this little girl's world, it was all about her. Someone wasn't talking to *her*, so there must have been something wrong with that person. She didn't get the person, so there had to be a way to figure her out, to get her to be like "the rest of us," she reasoned in her not-yet-mature brain.

Mean Girls aren't always mean on purpose, at least not in their minds. This little girl and her friends drove another girl to such pain that she had to move in order to be free from them, yet she saw no meanness in herself. The reason she didn't know she was being mean is that she was only thinking of herself and her own discomfort with a girl who didn't talk or act like her. She was oblivious to her own meanness until I confronted her with it. I'm still not sure she got it, since she was so absorbed in her own feelings, but we can hope that one day she will.

If you are the Outsider girl, you might like to learn more about why girls pick on you. Let's break it down to try to understand what in the world they're thinking. You haven't done anything wrong. You haven't done anything at all. All you've ever been is yourself. You might have a unique personality; you might be quiet, or shy, or even different-looking. But you aren't mean. You aren't even involved. You stay out of their lives, so why can't they stay out of yours? There may be any number of reasons why they chose you: maybe you are isolated, alone, and easy to attack, or maybe you are cranky, distant, or nasty back to them. But the real question is, what do you do? Take a look at this list and see if you can't change a few key things about your daily life that will help you be a less appealing target.

1. Don't be the easy enemy. Mean Girls feel bonded when they have a common enemy. And what they really want out of that enemy is lots of options for attack. In other words, they want easy targets, girls who can't defend themselves and have no one on their side. It's like when lions hunt: they pick the weakest animal of the herd, and that's usually the one that is separate from the others. So if you want to lose the Mean Girls, then get some friends. The less of a loner you are, the less of a juicy target you become.

2. Lighten up your attitude. If you're defensive, lighten up. Try not to react in anger, no matter what they do. If you can muster the strength to just be nice, you might find out that they change their tune when they're around you. Besides, you can't go your whole life thinking people are out to get you. If you do, then soon enough it becomes a self-fulfilling prophecy, and it happens only because it's what you planned for and reacted to. Expect more positivity from people and you just might get it.

3. Learn to love. Okay, I know that sounds impossible given the object of that love. You don't love them. You are scared of them. I know, I know, but who's bigger here? Your God or your Mean Girl? He says to love her, so that's what you gotta do. But we'll start slow, okay? No death-defying feats. Here's what I want you to do from now on, and you can practice it on your family members if you need to:

a. Look everyone in the eye when you approach them. It won't kill you, even though I know it will feel like it. But if you don't look into others' eyes, you can never love them.

b. Smile. Again, it won't kill you, but it might make you nauseous. You'll get over it, trust me. A smile is the best way to love on somebody. Your smile might be the only one some people get that day.

c. Go where the people are. Don't hide out. You were created to live in a community and to love others, not to be a hermit. That's hiding the love of God under a blanket where no one can see it. He is more important than that. Don't worry about yourself; worry about him. Is he being seen in you, or are you hiding him from a world that desperately needs him?

d. **Give people a break.** They are all hurting just as much as you, believe it or not, maybe just in different ways. Pray for them. Care for them. Show them you love them by noticing they exist. You aren't doing this for attention or for affection; you are doing this for God (see Galatians 1:10). So don't worry if they still make fun of you and don't get you. It will take time for them to adjust to your change. They haven't learned what you've learned, so they will need time to see you live it out over and over before they get the transformation. So don't fret.

Okay, so the Outsider is the easy target. She's all alone, usually a little defensive, and tons of fun for the Mean Girl to make squirm. But if that isn't you, then you are still scratching your head and saying, "Why are they picking on *me*?" Well, let's continue to explore.

THE POPULAR GIRL

Girls want to bond behind a common enemy, but it's not always as obvious an enemy as the loner girl. Lots of times they pick on the most popular girl or the smartest girl. Or even the most well-built girl. Why would they go after these kinds of girls? Ask me the same question and I'll tell you the same answer: because she's an easy target. Let's break it down.

You're popular; whether at school or work, people like you. But still this girl or gaggle of girls just won't leave you alone. They are relentless in slamming you and trying to make you look bad. Whassup with that? Well, it's because of your popularity that you became a choice target. The most popular people have always and will always be slammed by others because it's easy. No one wants to hear bad things about Joe Schmoe, but they sure love hearing bad stuff about celebrities or politicians. Unfortunately, it's human nature to want to hear bad stuff about people who are considered more successful than us. Something about it makes it easier to handle the pain of knowing that we aren't as popular as them. Jealousy and envy are some vile sins, if you ask me.

See, if a girl who is less popular than you can slam you good, then she gets a point, and that ups her hip factor. And the reason she can attack you is because so many others like her are just as jealous of you as she is, although they're probably not as mean since they're keeping their envy inside. So she knows right off she'll have an audience that will totally love what she has to say. Remember the *Globe* and the *National Enquirer*, those papers you see at the checkout stand? They make tons of money from unpopular (i.e., not famous) people who want to hear horror stories about the shortcomings of popular people (the famous ones). It's an industry. People will pay just to find out the latest gossip and half-truths. And it's no different at school or work, only what they pay is loyalty and friendship, not $1.95.

So don't be shocked if you are the target just because you are popular. It's the law of the jungle. So what do you do if you are popular and a target of a Mean Girl?

1. Invite her. Most of the time people pick on the popular girl because they are jealous. They feel unloved, left out, bitter. They are just hurt, and not really from anything you've done but from the thoughts that torture their own mind. So learn to care about them, to take note of them, and to invite them into your circle. It's really hard to be mean to someone who is nice to you all the time. Try this out on someone who isn't as scary. Next time you are at a restaurant or someplace where you are being helped by an unhappy or cranky person, say something nice to them. Compliment their necklace or tell them they have a nice smile. Say something that will make them show you that smile. A kind word can change a person's day and make them change their tune as well.

So practice being inviting next time you get a chance, and then go for it with the Mean Girl. Give her a nice card. Invite her to the movies. Buy her a coffee. I know this totally goes against what you want to do and what you feel is right, but oftentimes the right thing feels totally wrong. A lot of times the right thing goes against everything you've ever been taught, but check it out and see if it doesn't work. Or least check it out in Scripture and see if it didn't pay off for God's people:

- Abraham was told to sacrifice Isaac, his only son—it felt totally wrong, but obeying God turned out to be totally right (see Genesis 22).
- Noah was told to build an ark. Why? It appears as though it had never rained, let alone flooded the Earth. God's command seemed totally illogical, but Noah followed it and saved his family and the entire human race (see Genesis 6–8).
- Jesus allowed himself to be hung on a cross. It was completely horrific and unimaginable, and he begged his Father for another way, but doing it saved his people eternally (see Luke 22:42; John 6:40).

2. Talk her up. You've heard the expression "kill 'em with kindness." Well, now's your chance. An ancient proverb says, "If your enemies are hungry, give them food to eat. If they are thirsty, give them water to drink. You will heap burning coals on their heads, and the LORD will reward you" (Proverbs 25:21–22 NLT). Now, I know it looks like this proverb is telling you to burn your enemy, but dig a little deeper and you'll see that's not anywhere near the truth. In the days when this truth was written, people needed coals in order to keep their homes warm. If you were to give your enemy burning coals, then you would be warming them. You would be paying their heating bill. But why on the head? Well, you ever watch the Discovery Channel or read *National Geographic* and see those natives carrying sacks of rice, pots of water, and other heavy things on their heads? That is the way that many cultures carry things in the part of the world this proverb came from. So one possible explanation for this verse has to do with helping your enemy by giving them fuel for their furnace. But there is another explanation for this verse, and it makes just as much sense; in fact, it's like a one-two punch. The Egyptians had a tradition in the days when this was written that when someone was guilty, they would pile burning coals in a pan on their head and walk through town as a sign of repentance for what they had done. So the one-two punch of being nice to your enemy is that (1) it's what you are called to do and (2) it might actually lead them to saying they are sorry and to stopping the behavior, which is repentance. So with kindness you are loving your enemy, but that kindness can also help them to see the error in their ways.

I know what you're thinking: What an odd thing to do to your enemy—supply their needs, care for them? Seems (big word alert) preposterous! But again, illogical things are sometimes the most logical when you really look at them. Do something nice for your enemy, and they are no longer your enemy but your friend. It's hard to hate someone you are helping, and it's also hard for that person to hate you. This goes against everything the world has thrown at you, I know. But listen, the way the world has been doing it hasn't been working, so why would you want to copy the world? You've probably already proven its methods aren't working. For centuries girls have fought one another and grown into women who fight each other. If we want the madness to stop, we have to try something new by trying something old. Try the proverb and see if it doesn't prove true. Remember, if you keep doing what you've done, you'll keep getting what you've gotten. Is that good enough?

So what does this mean to you, Popular Girl? Well, what's the most important thing to most girls in high school? Their reputation. Bad reputation, bad life. Good reputation, good life, for the most part. So help her build her rep. Give her the gift of good gossip. Since you are the popular girl, you have the most power and maybe even the most responsibility to control social change in your school. What you say, people listen to. So here's what you can do. Tell people good stuff about the Mean Girl. Now, don't make it up, because you'll become unbelievable, but tell them things that are true. If you like her unique style, then tell people. If you think she has great hair, then tell people. Talk her up, make her look good to others, and help her to be elevated in the friend chain. She'll soon get wind of it and might not have a clue why you are doing it, and that will either shock her into kindness or freak her out so much she'll just leave you alone. In fact, if you are really brave, you could even try complimenting her when you know she can hear you. Nothing is better than overhearing someone talking nicely about you. It's addictive; you just want to hear more. So test the truth and see if it doesn't work.

Give her the gift
of good gossip.

Now, don't expect her to instantly want to be best friends with you. She might hate you for the rest of her life; you can't control that. All you can control is your own mouth, your own life, and your own destiny. Be the best you can be without worrying about if it changes other people, and you will win in the end. Even if her torture never stops, you win. So decide today who you want to be and then be that girl, not the girl she is trying to make you to be.

THE HOT GIRL

If you have a really nice body and have the guys' attention, watch out for Mean Girls. You'll be on the top of their list (as if you didn't already know that). Again, it's because you are an easy target. In fact, your existence almost begs them to harass you, because if they can make you look bad, then they come up a rung on the beauty ladder. It's just like your mother said: *"They're just jealous."* It's true, but that doesn't help you much, does it?

Okay, so they make the choice to hate you. But what's the solution? What can you do when you're too hot for the other girls? And before you say, "I'm not hot," let me just say that hot girls rarely *think* they're hot. But it's always what others think. And if you do think you're oh-so-hot, then you might want to tone down your self-appreciation just a bit. That might be what's making them all hate you. But if you are just hated because of your looks and you aren't parading around like a princess or supermodel, then what can you do? How can you cope?

1. Compliment them. First, know that you can't change them, you can only love them. (Note: love might make them kinder, but it's not your job to change them, only to love them.) If they feel insecure and ugly, you can't change that. No matter what you do. People's feelings are controlled by them, not you. So don't kid

yourself into thinking you can control a change in them. You can try to help raise their self-image, but you have no power over whether they accept it or not. But **just like the Popular Girl**, you the Hot Girl **pull some weight around your work or social circle.** You have power that you might not really be aware of. So saying something nice about the Mean Girl is a big win for both of you. If you haven't read it yet, go back and read "The Popular Girl" (page 83). Seriously, it will give you great ideas about reaching out to the Mean Girl. So stop now, go back and read, and I'll wait. It's way important!

2. Control yourself. You have the power to control yourself. You can decide what you are going to do about their reactions to you. If you've decided that you want to be the girl you were made to be, then you know you can't choose revenge. You can't take their anger and return it, because it's not gonna help you be the pure, good, faithful girl you were made to be.

3. Let it slide. Your only other choice is to let it slide. Think of yourself like a duck and their comments like water. You can swim right through them and they will never get through to your skin; they just slide off because you know their comments aren't true. This takes a lot of hard work and concentration, and some days you will think you just can't handle it any longer, but let me give you some hope:

God blesses the people who patiently endure testing. Afterward they will receive the crown of life that God has promised to those who love him.

James 1:12 NLT

Dear friends, don't be surprised at the fiery trials you are going through, as if something strange were happening to you.

1 Peter 4:12 NLT

If you think you are standing strong, be careful, for you, too, may fall into the same sin. But remember that the temptations that come into your life are no different from what others experience. And God is faithful. He will keep the temptation from becoming so strong that you can't stand up against it. When you are tempted, he will show you a way out so that you will not give in to it.

1 Corinthians 10:12–13 NLT

So you see, the Lord knows how to rescue godly people from their trials, even while punishing the wicked right up until the day of judgment. He is especially hard on those who follow their own evil, lustful desires and who despise authority. These people are proud and arrogant, daring even to scoff at the glorious ones without so much as trembling.

2 Peter 2:9–10 NLT

THE SHY GIRL

The Shy Girl is in an odd position because the way she acts looks a lot like the stuck-up Hot Girl. Think about it. The similarities are striking, not necessarily in outward appearances but in behavior. The stuck-up Hot Girl walks right by you and doesn't say a word, as if she's just too good for you. Shy Girl, you do the same—you walk right by and don't say a word to anyone. The stuck-up Hot Girl doesn't sit by people in class and just start talking to them, 'cuz she's too good for that, but neither does the Shy Girl. You just sit down and keep your eyes on your desk. Yeah, the stuck-up girl and the Shy Girl look a lot alike to Mean Girls. And that might be why they pick on you—not because you're shy but because they think you are just plain stuck-up. Mean Girls always think the worst. So when you don't smile at them, you avoid eye contact, and you never interact with them, they say to themselves, "She isn't very nice. She won't even smile at me. She must think she's too good for me." And their temperature rises. How could *you* think you are too good for *her*? You clearly aren't any better, she thinks, and *bam!*, she's off to prove it. It's simply a case of you being another easy target. You become, in her mind, a Mean Girl who needs to be taught a lesson. You need to learn to notice her like the rest of the world.

Now you, on the other hand, are just unbearably shy. You don't feel anywhere near as important or as good as the other girls, so you hide. You hide in a crowd, you hide all alone, you hide any way you can. You hide your eyes from theirs and your heart as well. I know, it's a big, dangerous world out there. And believe me, I know what it's like to be shy. In middle school and the first part of high school, I was the Shy Girl. I didn't know anyone in school because I had just moved to town in seventh grade. I didn't think anyone could possibly like me or want to talk to me, so I kept to myself. By ninth grade the girls assumed that I thought I was just too good for them, but that wasn't true at all. I was scared of them. I was insecure and unable to express myself. I came from a family of women who never interacted with other women. Having friends wasn't something we ever did. So I had no idea how to be a friend. And I was ostracized and made fun of by the more social girls.

Now that I'm older and can look back with less pain on my growing-up years, I realize that I could have done a few things differently that would have changed my life back then. One of them is that I could have known Christ, and that would have made a huge difference. See, knowing him would have meant that I could have confidence. Confidence that I was called to love others no matter how ill-equipped I felt. Confidence that life wasn't about me, it was about serving him and those he put in my life. The other thing I could have

done is that I could have gotten over myself and made more of an effort to make friends. I could have trusted Jesus enough to help me to find and nurture friendships. Oh, if I only knew then what I know now!

If you are a Shy Girl, I pray that you know Christ, because he really is your salvation, in more ways than one. It's simple, really: this amazing God sent his one and only Son to die for you so that all your sins, all your junk, would be forever erased. He sent him so that you could have direct access to the God of the universe. And with that salvation that he gave you by dying on a cross and covering up all your sins with his blood, you have been given a new set of rules to live by. You aren't the same girl you used to be. You have a bigger purpose. You have a mission. You were created for something, and now you know it. The world isn't about cliques and fighting. It isn't about who's the most popular or the smartest. It's about him. How can you serve him as a soldier and servant in his army? How do you come into the fullness of who you were meant to be, not who they are?

When you accept your position as a child of the King through the death and resurrection of Christ, an amazing thing happens: your agenda dies with him. It's called dying to self, and it's an amazing freedom. It's a set of wings that will allow you to soar high above these girls' pettiness and see your role in saving and serving them. You aren't alive to be hurt and fearful; you are alive to be a power in the world. You are alive to be used mightily by a living God. If you realize that he lives in you, and that he desperately loves these girls, then you begin to have the power to break out of yourself, to break out of being shy, and to love them the way he called you to. Remember, this life isn't about you and your fears; it's about your God and his plans for you. It's about loving him and loving them just because he loved you. So here's what I want you to do: I want you to power up. I want you to first realize who you are and then start to act like it.

"It is doubtful that God can use anyone greatly until he hurts them deeply."

—A. W. Tozer

1. Pray this with me: "Father, I am alone and lonely in this world. I have nothing in and of myself, and I know it. I have repeatedly failed in your sight and mine. But I'm thankful that you sent your Son to die a terrible death on a splintered cross just because you loved me so much. I accept that death and believe in the resurrection. I want to turn away from my bad ways and love you completely as Lord of my life. Thank you for designing me to be used in a big way by you. Thank you for loving me unconditionally. Today I accept that love and will walk in it. Thank you, Father. Amen."

2. To-do list. Now that we've gotten that taken care of, here is your assignment: I want you to learn about who your God is and who you are. No more lies, no more fears. You have a job to do, so it's time to get over yourself and start to love not only your friends but also your enemies. So get yourself a Bible and look up these verses. Write them down, learn them, and keep them with you always: Mark 12:29–31; Romans 3:22–24; Romans 8:15, 31–33; Romans 10:9; Romans 12:9–21; Galatians 5:24; Ephesians 6:12.

3. Fake it. Have you ever heard the term fake it till you make it? In this case it's what you've got to do. You've got to act like you are not shy in order to help those around you to get to know you. Think about it like this: how can you do what God commands, like reaching out to others and loving them if you are too shy to even look at them, let alone talk to them? Consider shyness an obstacle between you and obedience and refuse to let it define you. Break out and act as if you are the most confident person ever, and no one will know the difference.

THE SMART GIRL

What a burden intelligence is! You can't help it that you're smart, so how can they hold it against you? But they do. It all comes down to jealousy. It's an evil thing.* But it's a normal thing in a fallen world. People who don't know Christ as a best friend, who don't know Christ as their comforter and their protection, have only themselves to save them, and that's a scary thought. So when they see someone who has more than they have, they panic. They have to protect themselves, so they fight back. And if your Mean Girl is a Christian, then it's really too bad, because she should know better. Jealousy does not make God happy. It's against his law (see Galatians 5:26). And she should have enough hope in him not to need to attack you to make herself feel better. But alas, she doesn't, so now the question is, What do you do? You are smart; you can't change that, and who would want to? Smart is good.

But I wish there were a verse that said, "Be smart and do not sin." See, sometimes we can be so smart that we sin. And what I mean by that is that we are so smart that we allow our smartness to make us judgmental of others who aren't as smart as us. We don't have patience for people who just don't get it. Believe me, I understand this. I happen to be someone who gets stuff really quickly. I am a quick learner, and I admit that I've gotten very steamed at people who are slower than me. I mean, I got it, so why can't they? I huff and I puff, wishing they would hurry up and get it. I've hurt many of my friends and family members by being frustrated with their inability to get things that I already got, and that's just plain ugly. I have confessed this to them, and I am making every effort to avoid frustration with stupid people,

* Proverbs 27:4: "Anger is cruel and fury overwhelming, but who can stand before jealousy?"

but it's hard. See, I just called them "stupid," and they aren't! I'm just a tad quicker. And deep down I know that, but I make them feel stupid because I think I'm so smart.

Now, I'm not saying you're a little cocky. I'm not even saying you're Little Miss Smarty-Pants. Remember, your brains were a gift; most likely you didn't make yourself smart. But that doesn't mean that others won't resent you for it. So what can you do (besides shutting off your brain)? In some cases you might be doing everything right. You might not be huffy when others don't get it. You might not be a teacher's pet or Little Miss Know-It-All. (But if you are, then let me just say, Bingo! We found out why they hate you. Tone it down a bit!) They have no right to hate you, but hate you they do, so how will you cope?

Deep in the very nature of every human being are envy and covetousness. That's why God's law speaks against them. The reason they even have to be written about is that they're natural. What's not natural is the opposite—being happy for other people's gifts and caring about their happiness. Girl, you are in a unique position by being smart. It means that you can be used in ways that many others will never be used. You have the ability to comprehend things and achieve things that just might rock this world.

But if you spend all your time worrying about what other girls think of you, you will never get there. God has a plan for you, a purpose. He gave you a passion that burns deep in your soul that you aren't even aware of yet. I want to tell you two things about that passion. The first is that it's an amazing thing, and you should not let hate or meanness get in the way of doing what you were called to do. And the second is that you should never let your passion, your dream, get in the way of what you are commanded to do by God—and that is to love your enemies. Use your brain to figure out ways to help others. Don't make yourself dumber to help them. Help them at the same time that you help yourself. See, you have two missions: to live your passion for God and to love others. You can't give up on either. So use that big brain of yours and figure out how to love people who don't love you back. Start with this list.

1. **Look at what God has to say** about your enemy. Check out Exodus 23:4; Proverbs 24:17–18; Zechariah 7:10; Matthew 5:44; Luke 6:27; Romans 12:14; and Romans 12:20.

2. **Don't try to be the teacher's or boss's pet.** You alienate yourself from the rest of the girls around you when you constantly side with your teacher, coach, or boss. Try to love everyone equally, and don't get all wrapped up in being a "yes-girl." Keep connected with your peers.

3. **Help.** Help other people study or complete their projects. If you are smart, then give your time to help people who don't get it.

4. **Be comfortable with who you are.** If you are smart, then for the rest of your life you will probably face girls who hate you because of it. Don't act dumb to please them. Don't be mean. Just be who you are. In the end you will be honored and loved deeply by your God, and that is what really counts.

THE CONFIDENT GIRL

I always teach girls that confidence is one of the most beautiful things about a girl, and evidence of that is when Mean Girls hate you. If confidence wasn't so appealing, the Mean Girl wouldn't be jealous, but it is and she is. Confidence comes from a steady trust that God has you where you should be, when you should be there, and that he's got everything under control (go back to Romans 8:28!). It shows in your demeanor because you are at peace, and people are often jealous of that because most of them aren't at peace. Confidence isn't a bad thing; it's simply a recognition that you are who God made you to be and that is enough—no, that's more than enough. It's a beautiful thing, so others envy you for having something they don't.

So what can you do? Act insecure to please them? Cut yourself down? Complain about your big nose or wide behind? No, that would be dishonoring to the God who made your big nose and wide behind (see 1 Corinthians 6:19–20). Never give up your confidence for anyone, even if it will gain you access to the inner circle. It isn't worth it. But there are some things you can do. If you are confident, know that there will always be girls who hate you because you have what they desperately want. That never goes away, unfortunately. But you can try some things to help ease the pain.

1. Love 'em. If you are so confident, then it shouldn't be hard for you to do this one thing: love your enemy. Ugh! I know—how horrific but how holy. Read all about it in Exodus 23:4; Proverbs 24:17–18; Zechariah 7:10; Matthew 5:44; Luke 6:27; Romans 12:14; and Romans 12:20. Use your confidence to help others. Invite the Mean Girl over for a swim. Get to know her one-on-one. Help her with her homework. Do what you can to honor your God. She might not ever respond to your kindness, but this isn't about the outcome; it's about you serving your God the way he's called you to serve. Don't expect big changes in her but in you. You are the only one you can control. But risk this for your God—risk loving someone who hates you. And remember, love isn't about how you *feel*. God never commanded you to feel good about your Mean Girls (enemies), only to love them. Love isn't a feeling;

it is a choice. If it were a feeling, God couldn't have commanded you to do it, because feelings can't be ordered around.

2. React to her attacks with love, or at least humor. You are confident, so you can keep your cool when she attacks. If she says something mean to you, don't get mad. Just smile and say something funny (about yourself, never her), or else say nothing at all. Remember, you lose when she makes you mad. So no matter what, don't get mad.

As you can see, girls can hate other girls for all kinds of reasons. But regardless of why your particular Mean Girl decided she didn't like you, your reaction to her is clear. If you love God and you want to be obedient to him, then you have only one option, and that is love. Love can mean all kinds of things, but it is always selfless. Whatever form your love takes, remember that it's not about you and your image but about God and his hand in your life. Will you let the Mean Girl win and make you disobedient to God's call to love your enemy, or will you rise above her goading and prove yourself faithful?

Therefore, he who rejects this instruction does not reject man but God, who gives you his Holy Spirit.

1 Thessalonians 4:8

THE SPIRI-TUAL SIDE OF MEAN

MEAN THOUGHTS

In the movie *Minority Report*, starring our couch-jumping buddy Tom Cruise, the government of the future has developed the technology to read people's thoughts from a central location in the city. They use this technology to arrest future criminals before they ever even commit a crime. In this surrealistic play on a spiritual theme, they are able to judge people guilty of evil thoughts and to punish them before they do anything to anyone.

As I watched the film, I realized how much we take our ability to think private thoughts for granted, certain that no one would ever eavesdrop. How much would my thoughts change if I were judged for them as soon as I had them? What if what I thought, plotted, and planned actually had a consequence in some realm? The movie really got me to thinking.

"Crime
doesn't consist
in the deed
but in the will."

—Rufinus

Some 2,000 years before that movie, on the side of a mountain in Galilee, Jesus sat down with a bunch of his followers and began to explain truth to them. Can you imagine the scene? You can read it in the book of Matthew, chapter 5. As they watched him and hung on every word, he looked at them and said, "You have heard that it was said, 'Do not commit adultery'" (verse 27). Everyone in the crowd probably nodded and looked at each other in agreement. Jesus went on, "But I tell you that anyone who looks at a woman lustfully has already committed adultery with her in his heart" (verse 28). This probably shocked the audience. For them *thinking* had never been mentioned alongside of *doing* before.

Could he have meant it? Really? Is it really a sin to just think of sex with someone other than your spouse? Why not? If the police of *Minority Report* could see people's thoughts and intentions, how much more can God? You know that he is omniscient (all-knowing) and therefore knows everything you think before you even say it, right? *"Before a word is on my tongue you know it completely, O LORD"* (Psalm 139:4). So why wouldn't God convict you of your thoughts? To him they are no different than your actions. That's what Jesus told his disciples.

Are you sitting down for this one? He has more to say about your thoughts than just this stuff about sex. Did you know God says that when you have angry or mean thoughts about someone, you get the same punishment as a murderer?

> You have heard that it was said to those of old, "You shall not murder; and whoever murders will be liable to judgment." But I say to you that everyone who is angry with his brother will be liable to judgment; whoever insults his brother will be liable to the council; and whoever says, "You fool!" will be liable to the hell of fire.
>
> Matthew 5:21–22 ESV

So think about it like this: your thoughts are no longer secret. If you think you can let your mind wander or fantasize about what you are going to do to a certain girl, think again. You aren't alone in your head, even if it feels like you are. God's tuned in to all your thoughts—the good, the bad, and the ugly. How does that make you feel? Invaded? Scared? Loved? Think about it. He's involved in all your thinking. Are you happy about that right now? If not, then what do you want to do to change? Because he isn't going anywhere. He'll always be listening. Always taking note and responding to your thoughts.

I worked at a restaurant in Portland, Oregon. I was a server. It was a really busy place, and we worked our tails off. The thing that really shocked me, since it was my first restaurant experience, was how cranky all the servers were about their customers. Sure, they're nice to your face, but you'd never believe what they say behind your back. "That woman is driving me crazy!" one would scream. "I've never seen such an idiot in all my life," another would say. And the conversations went on like that all night. "I hate this guy." "I want to kill this woman." "Who does he think he is?" They rattled on and on. As I stood at the counter by the moaning staff, I did one of those daze things, like a dream sequence, where all the words just start to fade into each other and you think, *What is all this chatter?* And then suddenly it hit me: this must be what the world sounds like to God. All our complaining and moaning. All our evil thoughts and angry fantasies. He has to listen to everyone's bad days and cranky moments. How ungrateful we must sound to his giving ears. How miserable we are as we bring him into our pity parties and hissy fits. It's ugly, really, when you think about it. Noise pollution in the spiritual realm.

"It is **dangerous** for the mind to dwell on what is forbidden, to perform, and to plan out sin rashly. Even without carrying out our sinful desires, **what we will** is considered done. Therefore, it will be punished as an action. . . . Don't will it if you won't carry it out. By your mind's confession you condemn yourself."

—Tertullian

How much do you contribute to the noise pollution that God endures? What kind of stuff do you throw up to your Savior daily? Are your thoughts kind, grateful, and loving, or are they angry, hateful, and bitter? Which do you think pleases him most?

"Try to find out what is pleasing to the Lord."

—Ephesians 5:10 NLT

One of my favorite verses is Philippians 4:8. It's all about your thoughts—what they should be focused on. Paul tells the Philippians that they should think about good stuff, not bad stuff. Honorable, excellent, stuff like that. Now, as I see it, this is a good idea for two major reasons. One is that you are what you think. If you think nasty thoughts, you are a nasty person. If you think depressing thoughts, you are a depressing person. So you end up getting whatever you think most about. But the second reason is that God has to listen to your thoughts. And he takes them seriously. So if you want to honor him and please him, thinking good stuff is one major step on the way to doing that. So how about you?

- Are you proud of your thoughts?
- What do you think about most of the time?
- What do you think when you think about your enemies?
- Do you think more thankful thoughts or angry thoughts?
- If you could be convicted for your thoughts, what would you be convicted of?

In one way or another, my girls of God, in any one moment, you are the sum total of your thoughts. What you think about most tells you what you value, who you are, what you want, what you love, and all kinds of things. If I were to look at your thoughts, who would I see? Would you be proud? Answer these questions seriously and take some time to think about what you think about most.

Environmental Quiz

If you have realized that you are guilty of noise pollution, then you need to know that it's not only bad for the spiritual environment, it's also bad for your health. Those negative thoughts can make you depressed, lonely, angry, and a million other really bad things. Are you polluting yourself and the spiritual environment around you with your negative and mean thoughts? Let's take a quiz to see if we can't measure your negativity footprint.

1. When I lie in bed, I usually think about:
   (a) the bad parts of my day
   (b) how to get back at people
   (c) all the stuff I'm thankful for

2. When my mind wanders, it's usually stuck on:
   (a) thinking of ways to get revenge
   (b) worrying about stuff people did to me
   (c) the amazing God that I serve

3. Most of the time I feel:
   (a) depressed
   (b) bored
   (c) happy

4. My parents say that I'm:
   (a) a whiner
   (b) depressed
   (c) well balanced

5. When I'm with my friends, we mainly talk about:
   (a) how much we hate other girls
   (b) how miserable our lives are
   (c) how cool our lives are

6. At school/work:

    (a) there is at least one girl who hates me

    (b) there are several girls that I can't stand

    (c) there are all kinds of people, but I like them all

7. If God is listening in on my thoughts, he is:

    (a) not happy with me

    (b) not listening anymore 'cuz he's sick of me

    (c) proud of me

8. I want to change my thoughts and make them better.

    True   False

Scoring

Add up your points:

1. a = 1, b = 1, c = 3	5. a = 1, b = 1, c = 3
2. a = 1, b = 2, c = 3	6. a = 2, b = 1, c = 3
3. a = 1, b = 2, c = 3	7. a = 1, b = 1, c = 3
4. a = 1, b = 1, c = 3	8. T = 3, F = 1

8–18: Polluter! Take it easy on the negative thoughts! You don't have to be so down on everything. Remember, you are what you think, so you must be pretty miserable. If you want to feel better, try changing your negative way of thinking to a more positive one. It will be a hard change, but you can do it. I believe in you. Read over the next chapter, "Saving the Spiritual Environment," and see if you can't change the spiritual environment you are creating.

19–24: Environmentally sound. Congrats! Looks like you are taking care of your spiritual environment, keeping things clean and healthy. Keep up the good work. God is proud of you and so am I.

SAVING THE SPIRITUAL ENVIRONMENT

If you are a polluter—someone who treats your thoughts like a giant waste dump—but now you want to change, what do you do? How do you stop the spiritual pollution? The first step is to want to. That's the major hurdle for most people. They don't want to stop thinking bad thoughts because they like them too much. So deciding to stop is the first step. It's a step that Scripture talks about all the time. It's called *repentance*. And it's *a requirement in order to be forgiven*.

How's it done? It's easy. It's all about telling God what you did, how you hate it, and how you want to change. (Check it out in 1 John 1:9 and Proverbs 28:13.) You have to break yourself down enough to admit you were wrong. That's a biggie. You know how hard it can be to say, "I was wrong." Confession is just that—saying you were wrong. And it's a crucial part of changing your ways (repentance). So tell God how much of a jerk you've been, and then tell him thank you for forgiving you for it. Because remember, no matter what you have done, if you are a Christian, you are already forgiven as soon as you confess (see 1 John 1:9). It's the reason Jesus died (see Hebrews 12:2), and it's crucial to understand. So your job is to confess your junk and then thank him for the forgiveness his Word says you have.

> If we confess our sins, he is faithful and just and will forgive us our sins and purify us from all unrighteousness.
>
> 1 John 1:9

After you've gone through the confession, then you can get on to the renewing (see Romans 12:2). You've created a nasty habit of thinking bad thoughts. And habits take time to change. Just because you confess and are forgiven doesn't mean it all magically disappears and *bam!*, you're a new woman. Change is hard, and it takes effort. So here's the 411. You've gotta play mind police. Lay down the law, believe the law, and enforce the law. The law is just your list of things you are going to do or not do. You know your thoughts better than I do, so you can make your own law. Just base it on Philippians 4:8. What won't you think anymore? What will you think about?

> Finally, brothers, whatever is true, whatever is noble, whatever is right, whatever is pure, whatever is lovely, whatever is admirable—if anything is excellent or praiseworthy–think about such things.
>
> Philippians 4:8

> Do not conform any longer to the pattern of this world, but be transformed by the renewing of your mind. Then you will be able to test and approve what God's will is—his good, pleasing and perfect will.
>
> Romans 12:2

Next, enforcing the law. This is harder than it sounds, if that's possible. Now that you've agreed with God on what you will and won't let yourself think, it's time to keep yourself honest. The best way to do this is to stop yourself every time you start to think the wrong things. And the best way to do that is to say "no" out loud (or quietly under your breath, if other people are around). Just say "no." Your thoughts will be like, "What? You're telling me no? What's the meaning of this?" But don't worry. They'll get the hang of it. Now, once you've stopped the bad thought, you have to replace it with a good thought or it'll just come right back (see Matthew 12:44–45). The way to do that is to think something good, something holy. Pray for the person who's bothering you. Think of when you first met Christ. Thank God for something he has done for you—you shouldn't have to look too far to find something. Whatever you do, replace that ungodly thought with a godly one.

Remember, just thinking a bad thought doesn't mean you're bad; it just means you're tempted. If it did mean you were bad, then we would have to think Jesus was bad, and we know he wasn't. "For we do not have a high priest who is unable to sympathize with our weaknesses, but one who in every respect has been tempted as we are, yet without sin" (Hebrews 4:15 ESV).

Satan tempted Jesus with evil thoughts, but Jesus shut him down by saying no to them and replacing those thoughts with the truth (read how he did it in Matthew chapter 4). Scripture is your best weapon for fighting bad thoughts. So your job right now is to collect your weapons, just like Jesus did. Write down five verses that are truth you can hold on to when you start to think bad stuff. A verse like Romans 8:28 is good. Get all five verses onto cards or a sheet of paper you can carry around with you. You're gonna need 'em.

If you want a healthy and clean spirit and a loving relationship with your God, practice creating a clean spiritual environment by controlling your thoughts.*

"Good thoughts and actions can never produce bad results; bad thoughts and actions can never produce good results. This is but saying that nothing can come from corn but corn, nothing from nettles but nettles."

—James Allen

* For more help on this topic, pick up the book *As a Man Thinketh* by James Allen.

GETTING OVER IT

* "Jesus said, 'Father, forgive them, for they do not know what they are doing'" (Luke 23:34).

When it comes to the things that mean people do, a lot of time I hear girls say, "I was just so offended by what they said." Girls, this might come as a shock, but I am here to tell you that as a believer it is not okay to be offended. What? That's right. If you are offended by anything girls are saying *about you*, then you are caring more about self than about God.

Let me explain. If you are a believer, your goal is the same as mine: you want to be more like Christ. Right? I know that sometimes that seems impossibly hard; in fact, most of the time it is impossibly hard. But it's what you want to do. It's who you are. And what's more, it's what he wants you to do and who he made you to be. And in deciding to become more like Christ, one big thing that a lot of people miss when it comes to imitating him is that he was not offended for himself.*

In fact, only one thing offended him to the point of action, and that was when people offended his Father. Jesus had a lot of mean things done to him. People accused him of stuff he didn't do, beat him, put nails in his hands, and then told him to do something about it if he was who he said he was. They did everything under the sun to get a reaction out of him, but if you check out his life, you will see that the only thing that got him mad was when people offended the Father by misusing his temple (see Matthew 21:12–13). Those people weren't calling him names or punishing him unjustly; they were sinning against God, and he couldn't stand for it.

Just like Christ, you have a right to be offended when someone insults, abuses, curses, denies, or slams, in any way, your heavenly Father. More than a right, you have an *obligation* to take offense. But you don't have that same right when it comes to yourself—that is, not if you wish to imitate Christ.

To this you were called, because Christ suffered for you, leaving you an example, that **you should follow in his steps.** "He committed no sin, and no deceit was found in his mouth." When they hurled their insults at him, he did not retaliate; when he suffered, he made no threats. Instead, he entrusted himself to him who judges justly.

1 Peter 2:21–23

Think about this: People can slam you all day and call you what they will, and all the arguing in the world won't change them. And what do you care if it does? Are you now trying to please man, or God? If you are trying to please man, you are no longer pleasing God (see Galatians 1:10). Your goal is to honor your Father, to care more about him and what he says about you than about what they say. But part of honoring your Father is standing up for him. So if someone is offending the Father (sinning against him), then you have every right and in fact a duty to stand up to them. It's a fight for your God, not for yourself, because it isn't about you; it's all about him.

It's like this: Whenever I hear someone use the name of Jesus in vain, I get really offended. Not because it offends me personally (note: making me uncomfortable or mad is not a sin) but because it is an offense to him. It is an insult, a slam, a curse, and that makes me mad for him. But I also know that my wrath is nothing compared to the wrath Jesus showed when he threw over the money changers' tables. I don't have the power he had, but I do have his Word, and that's the next best thing to having him there in the flesh. So this is what I say: "Oh, I wouldn't do that if I were you—use Jesus's name as a cuss word. The Bible says it's a terrible thing to fall into the hands of the living God.** Be careful. I wouldn't want to insult God if it were me." Then I do something like shiver in fear and say, "Oooh, not a good thing."

I can't sit by idly while my God is insulted, but I can sit by while *I* am insulted, just like Christ did when he was hung on that cross.

** See Hebrews 10:31.

Not once did he fight back. Not once did he argue for himself (see Luke 23:9). Instead he trusted the Father to prove him right in the end, and boy, did he ever. So trust God with your reputation, and fight for his. When you are insulted, your only job is to ignore it or, as Jesus himself says, to "turn the other cheek" (see Matthew 5:39). And rest in the fact that "in all things God works for the good of those who love him" (Romans 8:28).

GET OVER YOURSELF

"If I had cherished sin in my heart, the Lord would not have listened."

—King David, Psalm 66:18

Your goal is to get rid of your Mean Girl, but God's goal might be to purify you. Either way, one question that you must consider when faced with a Mean Girl or any other mean person is, "Shall a part of me die because of her?" And the answer must be yes. As we've already seen, one big reason she might be in your life is to help you to learn to die to self. Death seems like such an awful and painful thing, and it can be both of those, but it is also a beautiful and necessary thing in the life of the believer. A symbolic death is on the lips of the apostle Paul when he says, "Those who belong to Christ Jesus have nailed the passions and desires of their sinful nature to his cross and crucified them there" (Galatians 5:24 NLT) and "So put to death the sinful, earthly things lurking within you" (Colossians 3:5 NLT). This death, this getting over yourself and nailing sin to the cross, is a thing of faith. And it can be just as painful as physical death and just as hard to accept. But we have to listen to the words of Christ: "I tell you the truth, unless a kernel of wheat falls to the ground and dies, it remains only a single seed. But if it dies, it produces many seeds. The man who loves his life will lose it, while the man who hates his life in this world will keep it for eternal life" (John 12:24–25).

What sinful parts of you might God be wanting you to crucify?

What kinds of things go through your heart and mind when you are attacked by a Mean Girl?

These bad thoughts and actions are the very things that need to die inside of you, and without this Mean Girl, how would you have seen into the dark recesses of your soul? So how can you use this girl as your chance to die to self and live for Christ?

Dead to Self, Alive to Christ

Dying to self means that you stop demanding that the world revolve around you.

Dying to self means that you give up the right to always be right.

Dying to self means that you turn the other cheek when someone attacks you and that you do all you can to live in peace, even if it means getting the raw end of the deal.

Dying to self means that all that is in you that isn't holiness and faith has to be denied.

1. Call it sin. The first thing you need to do is to identify what part of you needs to die: the sin part. What part of you has to be turned off, said no to, avoided, and even hated? These are the things that violate your spirit. These are the things that without God's grace you could not tackle. In other words, if you claim God's grace, put it to good use and tackle these things that up to now have controlled you. Agree with God that that stuff is sin, call it sin, and get busy getting rid of it, by God's grace.

"If God is anything, then He must be everything. And unless He is everything, He is nothing."

—Dick Woodward

The following is a list of reactions to Mean Girls that can derail a life of faith in an instant. Each one is followed by a verse reference so you can see it for yourself. God is very clear on what kinds of things drive you from his presence and damage your spirit. Know this list and avoid these things, even when it comes to your Mean Girl.

Fighting

Hostility—Galatians 5:19–21

Quarreling—Galatians 5:19–21

Anger—Colossians 3:5–10

Rage—Colossians 3:5–10

Malicious behavior—Colossians 3:5–10

Outbursts of anger—Galatians 5:19–21

Factions—Galatians 5:19–21

Divisions—Galatians 5:19–21

Always needing to be right—Galatians 5:26

Irritation with others—Galatians 5:26

Unforgiveness—Matthew 6:14–15

Keeping track of wrongs—1 Corinthians 13:5

Being happy when others are wrong—1 Corinthians 13:6

Foolish Talk

Complaining—Philippians 2:14; James 5:9

Foolish talk—Ephesians 5:4

Criticizing—Romans 2:1; 14:3

Passing judgment—Matthew 7:1–3

Slander—Colossians 3:8

Dirty language—Colossians 3:8

Lying—Colossians 3:9

Selfishness

Being conceited—Galatians 5:26

Selfishness—Philippians 2:3–4

Pride—Proverbs 18:12

Greed—Colossians 3:5

Idolatry—Colossians 3:5

Envy—Proverbs 14:30

Not Trusting Love

Giving up on love—1 Corinthians 13:7

Not trusting—1 Corinthians 13:7

Jealousy—Galatians 5:26

Fear—Isaiah 8:13

Unless you can die to those urges inside you for revenge, hate, and all the other things you allow Mean Girls to instill in you, your faith will be incomplete. Not only incomplete but disobedient, in fact. In his first letter to the Thessalonians, Paul writes,

"God has called us to be holy, not to live impure lives. Anyone who refuses to live by these rules is not disobeying human rules but is rejecting God, who gives his Holy Spirit to you"

(4:7–8 NLT).

2. Use the Mean Girl. Use the Mean Girl for good. Or should I say, let God use the Mean Girl. How? Well, when God asks you to die to self, the dying will be in something that you have to give up—something that you want to do, say, or be. It won't be giving up something that you *don't* want. God's not going to ask you to give up liver and onions if you don't want them in the first place. What would that prove? But if you really love getting revenge, he *is* going to ask you to give that up. Dying to self never involves doing something that's easy to do but always involves something that's a challenge. So don't shrink away from the Mean Girl as an obstacle in your path, but see her as your opportunity to learn more about dying to self.

"If your faith isn't changing you, it hasn't saved you."

—James MacDonald

3. Remember why you die. Every time you die to self, you are getting closer and closer to God.

It's like lifting weights—each time it hurts, you grow stronger and stronger. Remember that each time you hurt by reacting in a holy way, you become more and more like Christ. "For what credit is it if, when you sin and are beaten for it, you endure? But if when you do good and suffer for it you endure, this is a gracious thing in the sight of God. For to this you have been called, because Christ also suffered for you, leaving you an example, so that you might follow in his steps" (1 Peter 2:20–21 ESV). If you can remember that the goal is holiness, then each time you deny your urges, you will feel a life of faith growing in you.

"Since therefore Christ suffered in the flesh, arm yourselves with the same way of thinking, for whoever has suffered in the flesh has ceased from sin, so as to live for the rest of the time in the flesh no longer for human passions but for the will of God."

1 Peter 4:1–2 ESV

4. Be strong. When you practice dying to self, you will find that you actually become healthier spiritually and a stronger believer. You don't really die at all. Only the bad parts of you die. It's true, "everyone who exalts himself will be humbled, and he who humbles himself will be exalted" (Jesus in Luke 14:11 ESV). But a warning must come with this verse and that is that you can't use this idea of dying to self as an excuse to hurt yourself or neglect yourself in any way. Your body is a temple of the living God and it is important because of that. You are not worthless. You are valuable in God's eyes, so the only part of you that should be dying is the sinful part, not your confidence or your hope.

The next time you scream at God, "Why me? Why is this Mean Girl in my life?" think about this: his Word doesn't answer why *this* particular girl is in your life on *this* particular day, but it does tell you that you are called to a life of obedience. And that means obedience not just when obedience is easy but when it's the hardest thing you have ever done. If you really want to be obedient to God's Word, then read it. Find out all the things he asks of us; learn what you are called to do. I am doing this exercise myself and I would encourage you to try it with me, because it's hard to be obedient when you don't know what to be obedient to. Find every verse you can that calls you to *do* some kind of action or to *stop* some kind of action. I've given you a lot of them in this section. Go back and look them up if you haven't already. Put together a list of verses that applies to obedience in your life. Memorize them, keep them with you, and start to become ravenous for holiness. Strive for holiness like it's the most important thing in your life, and the Mean Girl will suddenly become just a blip on your radar screen. "For God did not call us to be impure, but to live a holy life" (1 Thessalonians 4:7). "Therefore, if anyone is in Christ, he is a new creation; the old has gone, the new has come!" (2 Corinthians 5:17). Put off the old, girls of God, and put on the new.

Hannah Sees the Truth

Lately, my Father has revealed to me a depth of selfishness in myself that I never even so much as suspected. I find that all my kindness to others, my benevolence, and what seemed to be the most unselfish acts of my life, all have had their root in a deep and subtle form of self-love. My motto has for a long time been "Freely you have received, freely give" and I dreamed that in a certain sense I was living up to it, not only as regards physical blessings, but spiritual as well.

But I find now that I have never really given one thing freely in my life. I have always expected and demanded pay of some kind for every gift, and where the pay has failed to come, the gifts have invariably ceased to flow. If I gave love, I demanded love in return; if I gave kindness, I demanded gratitude as payment; if I gave counsel, I demanded obedience to it, or if not that, at least an increase of respect for my judgment on the part of the one counseled; if I gave the gospel I demanded conversions or a reputation of zeal and holiness; if I gave consideration, I demanded consideration in return. In short I sold everything, and gave nothing. I know nothing of the meaning of Christ's words "Freely you have received, freely give." But I did it ignorantly.

Now however the Lord has opened my eyes to see something of the nature and extent of this selfishness, and I believe He is also giving me grace to overcome it in a measure. I have been taking home to myself the lesson contained in Matthew 5:39–48. I desire to do everything now as to the Lord alone, and to receive my pay only from Him. His grace must carry on this work in me for I am utterly powerless to do one thing toward it; but I feel assured that He will.

And I feel I have to thank Him for what He has already done. He has conquered a feeling of repugnance which was growing in me towards someone with whom I am brought into very close contact, and enabled me to give freely, without even wanting any return. Oh how great He is in strength and wisdom!

—Hannah Whitall Smith,
The Christian's Secret of a Holy Life

Obstinacy and self-will will always **stab Jesus Christ**. It may hurt no one else but your self, but it also **wounds His Spirit**. Whenever we are obstinate and self-willed and set upon our own ambitions, we are **hurting Jesus**. Every time we stand on our rights and insist that this is what we intend to do, we are **persecuting Jesus**. Whenever we stand on our dignity we systematically vex and **grieve His Spirit**; and when the knowledge comes home that it is Jesus whom we have been persecuting all the time, it is the most crushing revelation there could be.

Is the Word of God tremendously keen to me as I hand it on to you, or does my life give the lie to the things I profess to teach? I may teach sanctification and yet exhibit the spirit of Satan, the spirit that persecutes Jesus Christ. The Spirit of Jesus is conscious of one thing only—a perfect oneness with the Father, and He says "Learn of Me, for I am meek and lowly in heart." All I do ought to be founded on a perfect oneness with Him, not on a self-willed determination to be godly. This will mean that I can be easily put upon, easily over-reached, easily ignored; but if I submit to it for His sake, I prevent Jesus Christ being persecuted.

—Oswald Chambers,
My Utmost for His Highest

FIGHT-ING
MEAN

GETTING EVEN

"An eye for an eye and a tooth for a tooth." "If I don't stick up for myself, who will?" Getting even is just a little step in teaching the Mean Girl an important lesson, right? Or is it? Is getting even really such a bad thing? You're not a Mean Girl. You don't go around looking for a fight. You aren't bad. You're just a normal girl. If someone slams you or lies about you, how far is too far when it comes to evening the score? A girl has to protect herself. You can't just stand by while people walk all over you—that's your reasoning, anyway. Have a gander at this list and tell me your honest opinion. Which of these four situations can you relate to? And which are just going too far?

3-Way Call/IM—Your so-called "friend" is spreading rumors about you. You two are totally close, so you are completely shocked when you find out she's telling people that you are a loser. She is really nice to your face. You guys eat lunch together. You go to her house after work a lot. You're buds, so why is she doing this? It's best to just find out, isn't it? So you take matters into your own hands to find out what the heck is going on. Friday night while you are at her house you ask her, "Do you think I'm a loser?" She tells you, "Of course not! I think you're very cool. Why would you say that?" And you drop it because she's obviously not coming clean. But still you wonder. So on Monday you call up another friend and ask her if she will **do a 3-way call** with you so you can find out what's really going on. That night your second friend calls your first friend while you listen in. She starts talking about you and probing the other girl to find out what she *really* thinks about you.

Slam Book—A girl in your class has a smart mouth. She just loves to slam you whenever she gets the chance. She's funny, so everyone laughs at her. And by the way, they laugh at you too. How humiliating. So you decide to get even. You need a smear campaign that will totally prove to her that you are liked way more than her. So you start a petition. You get all your friends to sign a book or to post comments online that say all kinds of bad stuff about her. They all agree that she's a mean old hag and can't wait to sign on. Pretty soon you have pages full of hate comments agreeing that this chick is evil.

Smear Campaign—Your sorta friend totally stole your best friend from you, and now it's get-even time. It's not that you hate her, it's just that what she did was wrong, so you're gonna let everyone know about it. At lunch you start to tell all your friends what a cow she is and what a horrible thing she did. Then you go to the next table and tell all of them. You've started your own smear campaign. Just wait, she'll be sorry that she messed with you!

Blogging—The new girl in school took your spot on the volleyball team, and now she's moving in on your group of friends, getting all buddy-buddy with everyone, inviting them to do things without inviting you. You want to find a way to show them that she's mean and manipulative, so you write a story about the time she lied about you and made you look bad in front of the coach. You blog your little story about how horrible she really is for all to see.

The list could go on and on. Another girl does something to you, so you retaliate. It only seems fair. I mean, what are you supposed to do, just sit there and take it? If a girl starts it, then you're gonna finish it. But what tools do you use in your retaliation? When another girl starts something, what becomes fair game? Check all the things from this list that you'd like to use to get her back:

5   tell people what she did

5   3-way call on her

5   create a slam book

5   tell on her to an adult

5   get her in trouble

5   start a rumor

5   make fun of her

5   tell everyone how mean she is

5   TP her house

5   egg her car

5   slam her in front of your boss

5   tell your friends not to like her

5   other: _____

If you checked any of these and think that if she starts it, you can finish it, then let me ask you two simple questions: Has anyone done any of those things to you? Did it hurt? Don't just skim over this question. Think about it.

Did it hurt when someone did these things to you?

Was it mean when they did it?

If you would say, "Yes, it was mean when they did that to me," but you think it's still okay for *you* to do it, does that make *you* mean? Are you mean if you do mean things like these? Or are you just being you, and it's only mean when *they* do it? Think about that very carefully. You have to be honest with yourself if you want to face your own beast. Answer these questions and see where you sit:

1. How many times while you were reading this book have you had a memory pop into your head of a time when you faced a Mean Girl? _____

2. How many times while reading this book have you had a flashback of *you* getting revenge on a Mean Girl? _____

3. How many times have you 3-way called to get some info on someone? _____

4. Have you ever gossiped about a girl you didn't like?
   Yes   No

5. Do you know girls who really deserve to be put in their place?   Yes   No

6. Think about the girls in your life. Would any of them say that you had been mean to them?   Yes   No

Now, I believe in you. I don't think that you want to be mean. Maybe you just didn't realize that you were mean. Unfortunately, it's part of girl world to fight with each other. It's a dog-eat-dog world out there, and you have to protect yourself. Believe me, I understand. But since I know that you don't want to be mean and that you do want to be holy, let me help you out on this. To be mean simply to protect or stand up for yourself is still being mean. And not only is that bad but the revenge part itself is dangerous territory. It's stealing. Yep, you read it right, revenge is stealing.

And it's not just ordinary stealing—it's stealing from God. Eek! Not a good thing. Not someone to mess with.

See, in his Word God says, "Vengeance is mine." Oops, did you miss that? Check it out: in the book of Deuteronomy, chapter 32, verse 35 in the New King James Version of the Bible, God says, "*Vengeance is Mine.*" And in *The Message*, a paraphrase of the Bible by Eugene Peterson, the same verse says, "*I'm in charge of vengeance and payback.*" Did you catch that? It's God's job, not yours, to get even with people. The second that you go for revenge, you steal from God by taking the vengeance that is his. And think about this: revenge is defined as an opportunity for getting satisfaction, for getting even. The moment you seek revenge, you are self-seeking. You are looking out for yourself and trying to get satisfaction. That flies in the face of all that is holy, righteous, and good. Perhaps you don't know this, but as a child of God you are called to:

> sacrifice yourself (Romans 12:1)
>
> think of others rather than yourself (Romans 12:10)
>
> take care of your enemies (Proverbs 25:21)
>
> love your enemies (Matthew 5:44)
>
> not repay evil with evil (1 Peter 3:8–9; Proverbs 20:22)
>
> trust God to judge (1 Peter 2:23)
>
> forgive (Proverbs 17:9)

If you still think you have a right to revenge, then please explain. In the space below, write down how revenge fulfills any of the callings I listed above.

My revenge is holy because _____
_____ .

vengeance = punishment inflicted in retaliation for an injury or offense

revenge = an opportunity for getting satisfaction; i.e., you taking God's job away from him

If you want to stop the cycle of mean, then start today. Write down why revenge is evil and then make a commitment to never again seek what isn't yours.

Revenge is evil because _____
_____.

My commitment: _____
_____
_____.

Revenge is defined as an opportunity for getting satisfaction, for getting even. The moment you seek revenge, you are self-seeking.

If you want to let God have his vengeance back, you think he can do it better than you anyway, and you want to be a holy girl, then read this prayer out loud right now:

Father, today I commit to being holy. I choose to follow your Word rather than my emotions. I will not be self-seeking. I will love those who hate me. And I will trust you to take care of the situation. I will overlook offenses, and I will practice love rather than retaliation. I want to stop the cycle of mean. I want you to be proud of me. I want to be proud of myself. Thank you for forgiving me for all the mean stuff I have done in my life. Today I make a clean break. Today I will learn to love the world the way you do.

If you prayed this out loud, then good for you. I know it's hard to say that you've been mean, so I'm proud of you for admitting it. That's the first step in stopping the cycle of mean. From now on ask yourself, *Do I want to love or hate? Is this from the Father or from the enemy?* If you choose love, God will help you through the trials that the other girl has brought you into. Trust him and he will make you holy.

STANDING UP TO YOUR MEAN GIRL

The LORD your God is with you,
he is mighty to save.
He will take great delight in you,
he will quiet you with his love,
he will rejoice over you with singing.

—the prophet Zephaniah, from the book of Zephaniah 3:17

If getting even with the Mean Girl is out, then what about standing up for yourself? At least you can do that, right? Most self-help books on the topic of mean will tell you to definitely stand up for yourself. After all, you have to protect yourself, fight for your rights, and not become a doormat. And that sounds really good. But standing up for yourself is a delicate task and not one to be taken lightly or without much preparation. As believers we must go about confrontation much differently than nonbelievers.

With that said, let me explain what standing up to the Mean Girl is not. It's not getting in her face. It's not arguing back, putting her down, or attacking her. That's not standing up to her. Standing up to a Mean Girl is really standing up for your promise to please God over yourself. As a believer, you stand up in the face of attack by removing yourself from the attack, either by saying something positive or by just walking off. If you get in her face to fight for yourself, you lose sight of God because her face obscures your view. But if you stand up to her in order to please God, he is between you and her, and he is still your focus. So when you stand up to her, be sure that you are doing it to please God, not yourself.

While you live in the land of Mean Girls, I want you to understand that you aren't the victim; you are the faithful one. You aren't their prey; you are a lover of enemies. When you can see

yourself as a tool in the hands of God rather than a target in the eyes of the Mean Girl, you win!

WHO ARE YOU STANDING UP TO?

Before you get out there and start standing up, you've gotta note one more subtlety: how you talk to a believer and how you talk to a nonbeliever are really different. They are not coming from the same place, so you need to approach them according to different standards. Let's break it down.

STANDING UP TO NONBELIEVERS

Nonbelievers are a different animal than believers simply because they don't live according to God's law or they're completely ignorant of it. Therefore they can't be confronted with God's law, because it will mean nothing to them. As believers we shouldn't be surprised by the cruel acts of nonbelievers; they do them because they are ignorant or unrepentant, refusing to live by God's law. So know that if you attempt to confront them with "sin," you will be throwing pearls before swine, because they won't understand you. Instead you are to follow the precept of loving your enemy. And remember, love isn't a feeling, because a feeling cannot be commanded, and love *is* commanded. Therefore love is simply an action that we do no matter how we feel.

If you feel compelled to stand up to a mean nonbeliever, know that it probably won't change her, but as I've said before, if you don't cave and get all freaked out, then she is less interested. Here's an example: if she is spreading lies about you, calling you a cheater and threatening to tell your teacher some big lie, you can say something like, "Okay, that's fine. The truth will be known. Do whatever you like." And then leave. Remember, you aren't sent by God to call her on the carpet for her sin when she is unaware of what sin is. Convicting her is the job of the Holy Spirit, not you (see 1 Corinthians 5:9–13; John 16:8). But you can stand strong by letting her know that you won't be her victim or pawn. How? By simply not breaking under her pressure. Remember that it doesn't matter what she says or thinks—only what God says or thinks.

Standing up often means not giving in to her attempt to make you mad and not giving in to your urge to get even. Standing up means standing on your faith that everything will be okay because it's all under God's control. It also can mean refusing to be manipulated or made scared by her. Standing up can be many things, but, I repeat, it is never violent, hateful, confrontational, or hurtful. Standing up is simply being aware of who you are and making sure she knows you don't need her approval or love to be whole. It's confidence in your faith and your God.

STANDING UP TO A BELIEVER

Believers, on the other hand, are held to a higher standard by God, and therefore you can talk to them about God's commands such as love and kindness. But as I will say several times in this section, that may not always be the best option for you at the moment. For one thing, it is important that we, as believers, hold one another accountable, but it also is important that we understand that some girls who call themselves believers might actually be lying to themselves and to you. In that case, whatever you say about faith might fall on deaf ears, so don't be surprised. But if she is a true believer who really wants to serve God, then hearing from you might be just the thing she needs to turn her life around.

RECONCILATION

If you are offering your gift at the altar and there remember that your ~~brother~~ a Mean Girl has something against you, leave your gift there in front of the altar. First go and be reconciled to your ~~brother;~~ a Mean Girl then come and offer your gift.

Jesus (in Matthew 5:23–24)

According to God's Word, there are two times when you might go to a sister in Christ who's shown she has something against you or against God's call to love you. One is described in Matthew 5:23–24. In this instance, notice that Jesus tells you that if *she* has something against *you*, you are to go and work it out. If your Mean Girl is a believer, it is up to you to go to her with the issue. This might mean apologizing for what makes her mad or loving her in spite of her attitude. It isn't pointing your finger at her, getting in her face, calling her a name, or trying to fix her. This isn't permission to be holier-than-thou. It's a call to love one another and not let problems ruin friendships. So only pull this verse on a sister in Christ. Only use it when you know that there is something you can do to help the situation—that is, to bring reconciliation. (Note: The word *reconcile* means to restore to friendship or harmony. So whatever harmonious or good relationship you had before she got mad at you is the relationship you try to get back to. You might keep in mind that if she was never your friend to start with, you can't expect to be restored to a great friendship, because you can't restore what you never had.)

CONFRONTATION

If another believer sins against you, go privately and point out the fault. If the other person listens and confesses it, you have won that person back. But if you are unsuccessful, take one or two others with you and go back again, so that everything you say may be confirmed by two or three witnesses. If that person still refuses to listen, take your case to the church. If the church decides you are right, but the other person won't accept it, treat that person as a pagan or a corrupt tax collector.

Jesus (in Matthew 18:15–17 NLT)

This was a Jewish custom: when someone sinned against God and a believer was aware of their sin, he was to confront them privately. It was really an ugly embarrassment as well as a sin to bring other people into the situation unless it got really out of hand. The godly thing to do was to talk to them privately, not to punish them but to help bring them back into a right relationship with God. The translation of "sins against you" was more than likely not part of the original text. The idea is that someone sins against God by doing something to you. Their real sin is always against God but oftentimes perpetrated on you. That's part of the reason why you have no right to revenge. It's God's job, remember, to punish and judge. If the sinning sister didn't see the error of her ways, then Jesus said that you should take one or two other people who knew of the sin as well and confront her to bring her to repentance. Then if she still refused to admit she had done anything sinful, he said that the church should be brought in to do kind of an intervention, confronting her on her sin and hoping that would finally jolt her into the reality of her ways. In the end, if the girl was still numb to her sinfulness, she was to be kicked out of the church, again in the hopes that this would really knock some sense into her.

Now, before we go any further, let me throw out a major note of caution. I mention this verse because I want you to know Scripture, but when I was younger I found it very hard to separate my emotions from the problem. And if I had taken this verse as a call to action, I would have ended up making the Mean Girl madder than she was over something that wasn't that big of a deal. Because if you aren't completely emotionally detached you're gonna come off as holier-than-thou and using God's Word to get revenge.

Never use the Word of God to manipulate or get even with people.

This verse is tricky, and a lot of people use it too cavalierly. Be very sure that God is calling you to take this girl to the mat spiritually. Be careful that you aren't being overly judgmental or sensitive. This verse is for serious sin that *must* be confronted, so tread lightly here. Remember, you are called to turn the other cheek. If you obsess about teaching her a lesson or proving her wrong and your motives are impure, then beware, God will not be pleased. This is why I suggest that your first reaction should be to ignore her attack and love her. You don't know where she is in her faith, and you can't be sure that she even chooses to live by faith, so use this verse only in rare situations. If you use it every time you feel slighted, you will begin to abuse it, and you will find that the attacks will be even stronger and the name-calling will turn toward your holier-than-thou behavior. Talk to God before you attempt to use this verse. Ask him if his call to you is to die to self rather than to cure the Mean Girl. Ask him, "Is what she did a sin against you?" Does he call what she is doing a sin? If you think that she has sinned against the Father, how would he have you remind her? Is confrontation a good idea? What verses in the Bible say that she has sinned against God? Be sure you are on solid footing before you go to her about what seems to be a sin.

Verse Note: This is a verse on church discipline. How many times have you seen this done in your church? If mature Christians are not using this at every drop of the hat, then you better check yourself. It isn't something to be taken lightly. So tread carefully.

THE HOW-TO'S OF CONFRONTING

Now, if you still feel compelled to say something, you should do it when she is alone so she doesn't get embarrassed in front of her friends. Also remember to do it in love, not judging or condemning her and not telling her what she did to *you*. Take yourself out of the equation. If you can't take yourself out of the equation because you are upset, then wait until you can. And finally, remember, your job is not to change her or punish her; it's just to remind her of God's law and her trespasses against it. (Note: Because this is such a serious approach, please beware of sounding "holier-than-thou." Any attempt to criticize or judge could only make things worse. Whatever you do, do it in love.) She might not really have realized what she is doing. When she does, she might ask for forgiveness right away, but don't demand that in response to your following God's law. Your job is to obey him, not to demand that she does as well.

Check yourself: If it's a serious sin against God, then think about discussing your situation with a neutral adult (i.e., not your parent or boyfriend) who can shed light on things and see in you whether your motives are pure before you bring this up to the Mean Girl. (Note: don't have the adult do it for you.) And don't let this verse distract you from the more likely response God might be calling you to give: forgiveness and grace.

I know I have said "be careful" and "check yourself" a lot in this chapter, but when it comes to standing up, you really do need to do those things. Standing up is used in rare instances, because most of the time turning the other cheek is more appropriate. In everything that you do, make sure that your motives are pure and that you are only doing what God's Word, not your emotion, calls you to do.

Standing Up for Others

"Take tender care of those who are weak."

1 Thessalonians 5:14 NLT

While you aren't called by God to stand up for yourself, you are called to stand up for others. If you see a girl who is a victim of Mean Girls, then you can and should do something. Remove her from the situation, bring in the troops, surround her with friendly faces, call the Mean Girl on her lies. Stand up for the weaker—that's what we are called to do. But that doesn't mean you pick a fight or you act out of anger or retaliation; it only means you do what you can to be a peacemaker. *"God blesses those who work for peace, for they will be called the children of God"* (Matthew 5:9 NLT). Love both the victim and the Mean Girl and do what you can to defuse the situation. If you aren't sure what to do, then get someone in authority, like a teacher or counselor, and ask them to help. Research conflict resolution to find out how to help a bad situation. Just don't turn the other cheek to pain happening to someone else, but don't become a Mean Girl yourself in rescuing your weaker sister. *"Do for others as you would like them to do for you"* (Luke 6:31 NLT). Do what you can to make a difference and be a peacemaker.

MEAN FRIENDS

Mean Girls aren't always your enemies—sometimes they are your friends. If you have been feeling a little or maybe even a lot of mean coming from your own friend, it's time to ask yourself a few questions about the mean in your life. Let's start with a quick quiz.

IS YOUR FRIEND A MEAN GIRL?

Do you feel worse after hanging out with your friend?
   Yes   No

Do you have to be careful about what you say when you're with her?   Yes   No

Can you call her when your world falls apart?   Yes   No

Does she get jealous when your life goes well?   Yes   No

Does she get mad when you tell her no?   Yes   No

Does she make you feel guilty when you won't do what she wants to do?   Yes   No

If you answered yes to most of these, your friend might be a Mean Girl.

10 CLUES YOUR FRIEND IS BAD NEWS

She's your best friend. You do everything together, but you just don't think you like her anymore. Maybe she's changed lately, or maybe you've changed. Either way, she's driving you crazy, and you don't know what to do, but you don't want the grief any more. It's awful, I know. Let me be the first to tell you that it is okay to break up with your friends. In fact, you have the choice to stop being friends with anyone you don't want to be friends with anymore.

As believers we are always told to love people, and we should. But loving people doesn't always mean being friends with them. Sometimes being friends with them is actually harming both them and you. So step back and figure it out. If you've read some stuff in this book that makes you think your friend is a Mean Girl, then it might be time for a friend change.

Double-check this list to see if she fits any of these. If she does, ask yourself if you are being faithful by allowing her to be mean.

1. *She's overly defensive.* You can never tell her if she does something wrong, 'cuz she just flips out.
2. *She loves to talk about other people.* If she spends most of her time talking about other people, then beware, because she's probably talking about you when you aren't around.
3. *She loves revenge.* Don't ever cross her, because she'll get even. She doesn't let anybody get her. She's revenge central.
4. *She's religious, not spiritual.* She lives by a strict list of right and wrong, and if you don't agree with her, she judges you. Sometimes she acts so holier-than-thou that she sounds like one of those Pharisees Jesus talks about. Be careful not to hang out with a fraud, or your faith will begin to suffer.

5. *She's always gotta look good.* If she's scared to look stupid, then she's probably really cranky when she does something stupid. Mean Girls don't want to be laughed at, and if they are, their anger flares.

6. *It's all about her.* If she doesn't care about how other people feel, then she's not a safe friend.

7. *She always flatters you.* Flattery feels great, but when it's all someone does, you might start to wonder what they want from you. Friends are people who can be honest with you and don't always have to stroke your ego to make you like them.

8. *She never forgives.* Forgiveness is a command from God. Don't forgive and you won't be forgiven, and a soul that can't forgive is a soul that isn't faithful to God's Word. If she never forgives and never forgets, then she might be making your life miserable.

9. *She's jealous of your wins.* If she can't celebrate with you when things go great for you, she might just be jealous. Jealousy is a dangerous beast and can flare up in many different ways. If she tends to prefer it when you are miserable, she isn't a true friend.

10. *You feel worse after talking or being with her.* Friends should make us feel better, not worse. If you feel bad after being with her, something is wrong. Whether it's something she does or something she says, you shouldn't consistently feel worse after talking to a friend.

If your friend is a believer, then you can talk to her about her meanness. But be sure to do it in love. Don't judge her or whine to her. Treat her as you'd like to be treated. She might not even realize what she's doing. Or she might freak out on you, but either way, it's only fair for you to tell her what she is doing that is wrong. Read "Standing Up to a Believer" if you need more help on working things out with your mean friend, but also know that being friends isn't a free pass on mean. Friends put up with each other's junk, it's true. We forgive and (usually) forget, but if your friend has a habit of being mean and it's affecting your life, then it might just be time to break up with her. Turning the other cheek is the method for handling girls who are mean to you, but that doesn't mean that you come back begging for more day after day. You can easily stay out of her mean way by cutting back on time together. As a believer, she should not be making your life miserable, and separating from you might just be what she needs to push her to do something about her meanness.

THE BATTLE ISN'T AGAINST FLESH AND BLOOD

I know you think your fight is against a girl. I know she's the one who is the thorn in your flesh right now, digging in and causing you all kinds of pain, but remember that things aren't always as they seem. And if you want a life filled with spiritual victories, then you've gotta learn one important thing: *you aren't fighting the girl, you are fighting the enemy.* Paul makes this totally clear in his letter to the Ephesians. Check this out.

> A final word: Be strong with the Lord's mighty power. Put on all of God's armor so that you will be able to stand firm against all strategies and tricks of the Devil. For we are not fighting against people made of flesh and blood, but against the evil rulers and authorities of the unseen world, against those mighty powers of darkness who rule this world, and against wicked spirits in the heavenly realms.
>
> Ephesians 6:10–12 NLT

See, you aren't fighting her, really. She's just the decoy, the thing that distracts you from the real issue. So take your eyes off of her, and let's get back to reality. It's like that movie *The Truman Show*, where Jim Carrey's character has no clue that he lives on a movie set and that everything he is doing is directed and planned by the show's producers and directors. It isn't till he steps outside the set that he can start to see the fakeness of all that he thought was reality. Take a look behind the scenes, just like Truman did, and see if you don't find out who's really pulling all the strings, writing all the lines, and making the mean actors play their parts. Don't hate the actors; hate the director who is directing them to be mean to you. For those of you who are having a blonde moment and have no idea who I am talking about, I mean Satan, the devil, the dark ruler of this earth. Check out 1 John 5:19 and 1 Peter 5:8–9. He's really the problem here—the director of evil.

STAND FIRM

So if you aren't supposed to go after the actors, who do you go after and how do you do it? Well, first of all, let's figure out our role in God's army. As I see it, we are never called to be on the offensive. We are only to defend. We defend our God, we defend the less fortunate, and we can defend ourselves against the attacks of the evil one, but never do we go in and pick a fight. It's called standing firm. You have three options in a fight: you can run away, you can go on the offensive and attack, or you can stand firm. Your call is to stand firm in who you are, what you believe, and Christ's commands to love your enemies. Remember that with him you are victorious. If you stand firm on a foundation that can't shake, then you don't have to run or attack, because you can simply stand. Jesus said, "By standing firm you will gain life" (Luke 21:19). And the apostle Paul tells us in his 1 Corinthians 16:13, "Be on your guard; stand firm in the faith; be men of courage; be strong." In order to stand, you are called to be armored up and protected. That's why in Ephesians, Paul talks about us putting on the protective armor of God. We are called to suit up to protect our important parts—our minds, our hearts, and our feet. Check it out:

Therefore put on the full armor of God, so that when the day of evil comes, you may be able to stand your ground, and after you have done everything, to stand. Stand firm then, with the belt of truth buckled around your waist, with the breastplate of righteousness in place, and with your feet fitted with the readiness that comes from the gospel of peace. In addition to all this, take up the shield of faith, with which you can extinguish all the flaming arrows of the evil one. Take the helmet of salvation and the sword of the Spirit, which is the word of God. And pray in the Spirit on all occasions with all kinds of prayers and requests. With this in mind, be alert and always keep on praying for all the saints.

Ephesians 6:13–18

Your first step in fighting the real enemy is to suit up. Put on the right outfit to get ready for battle. You've gotta have the right clothes on for the right occasion. I mean, you wouldn't go to school in your bathing suit or to the beach in your school clothes. And you don't go into battle without your spiritual armor. You can and should put it on every day. And I know you may have heard this a million times, but have you ever heard *how* to do it? It's not like you have a closet at home with all this stuff in it. So let's go over the list and how you put this stuff on. Every day you should ask God to dress you up in the following:

The helmet of salvation—The helmet protects your thoughts from the arrows the enemy will throw at you. Stuff like, *You aren't good enough for God. He'll never forgive you for that. You have to work harder to make him love you. How do you even know he exists? Have you ever seen him?* If you've ever had thoughts like these, then you need the helmet of salvation. It protects you by letting you know that you are saved, period, no matter what you do or how you do. No matter if you mess up or anything. You are saved, period. So with the helmet on, this tactic from the enemy is kaput.

The breastplate of righteousness—The breastplate was a defensive weapon that men wore in Bible times. Think of it like a metal corset. It protects your most important part, your heart. When the enemy starts to come at you with all kinds of lies about how bad you are, the breastplate stops that nonsense from getting into your heart. See, you *are* righteous just because Christ made you to be, not from anything you've done. God said there is no one righteous, not one, on their own (see Romans 3:10). But you are righteous because *he* is righteous and *he* made you that way (see Romans 3:22). So Satan is lying when he tells you that you are no good. The breastplate of righteousness reminds you of that important fact.

The shield of faith—When a soldier went into battle, he always had a shield with him. That's the thing he held in his hand to deflect blows from spears, sword, and arrows. For believers our shield is our faith. It deflects all kinds of weapons from the enemy. Faith is what makes us win. It's what reminds us that we *do* win because Christ made it so (see the second half of 1 John 3:8). Without faith, don't dare go into battle, because you will certainly lose. Faith that God will protect you, that he works everything out for good, and that he is in control protects you from all kinds of stuff.

The belt of truth—The next little piece of apparel is your belt. It's essential. The belt of truth reminds you what's true, because the enemy's biggest weapon is the lie. He uses lies very masterfully to deceive you. He makes them look really close to the truth, but they're off just enough to mess you up royally. If you have the belt of truth on, you will be able to distinguish the truth from a lie. And you won't fall for the lies of the enemy anymore (see 2 Corinthians 11:14 and John 8:44).

The sandals of the gospel of peace—The most important thing for us to know as believers is the gospel, the message of Jesus. Do you know the gospel? Can you tell someone the gospel on cue? It's crucial that you can. It's what saves you and everyone else on earth. Make sure that you know the gospel: the truth that "there is no one righteous, not even one" (Romans 3:10), and because of that, a sacrifice had to be made for our sins. Christ was that sacrifice, once and for all. He died for our sins, even though he was sinless, so that we could have a right relationship with God. Without his death on the cross and resurrection, none of us would be saved. The old, some say overused, verse John 3:16 is not just a cliché.

The sword of the Spirit—No warrior would be complete without his sword. This is used for hand-to-hand combat with the enemy. When they are in your face and you need to react to protect yourself, you pull out your sword. As a believer, your sword is God's Spirit, or his Word. You have to protect yourself with God's Word. The stuff he says in Scripture is so powerful that it can destroy the enemy. Don't just believe me; give it a try yourself. The next time you are thinking stupid or negative thoughts, pull out your favorite Scripture. Read it over and over again. Let the enemy know that he's a loser, you're the winner. Your team wins, and you are sure of it. The sword is a must if you want to fight the battle against the enemy.

Every morning before you leave the house, put on the right outfit. Make putting on your spiritual outfit more important than anything else you do. It doesn't take long. Just pray something like this:

> Father, this morning I want to put on the armor of God. I want to put on the helmet of salvation so that I will remember that I am saved for good and no one can take me away from you. It's permanent, this salvation thing. Thank you, Father. And I also want to put on the breastplate of righteousness. I know that I am righteous because you say I am. I am righteous because your Son died for me to make me righteous (as Romans 4:22–25 says). I won't let the enemy lie to me about my sins

or my faults, because it's none of his business. Next I want to put on the belt of truth around my waist. Your Word is true, and I know the truth will protect me. Today I will not tell myself lies or even let myself think about them. I'll only think what's true and excellent and good (as it says in Philippians 4:8).

Father, please put the sandals of the gospel of peace on my feet so that I will remember to tell those who don't know you the truth that Christ's death on a cross meant something. It meant that you loved each of us enough to give your Son for us. And because of that, nothing anyone says or does to me today will derail me. Thank you for the gift of the gospel.

The Gospel =

1. God loves you and has big plans for your life (see John 3:16; John 10:10).
2. Man is sinful, so man can't get close to God, who is all good (see Romans 3:23; Romans 6:23).
3. Jesus died and rose again so that we can get to God. He makes us righteous. He is the final sacrifice for each of us (see Romans 5:8; 1 Corinthians 15:3-6; John 14:6).
4. If you accept Christ as your sacrifice and make him Lord, then you can know God and live the big plans he has for you (see John 1:12; Ephesians 2:8-9; John 3:1-8).

Adapted from *The Four Spiritual Laws*

Father, I pick up the shield of faith and carry it with me no matter where I go today. My faith is secure. You are who you say you are, and no one can make me budge with the shield in my arms. Thank you for your protection for those who love you (shown in 1 Peter 1:5).

And last but not least, I'm picking up the sword of the Spirit to help me fight the enemy at every turn. The sword that you give me is your Word, the Bible. I will take it with me no matter where I go. I will learn verses that I know can fight the enemy, and if I can't remember them, I will write them down so I can take them wherever I go. Thanks for the protection and power of your words (as Isaiah 54:17 shows).

Thank you for the protection of your armor. Amen.

If you put on the armor of God every day, just like Paul teaches us in God's Word, then you will feel God's protection on you all day long. It's a good reminder of what is important too. If you can just remember the big stuff, like Jesus dying because of how much he loves you, then the other stuff gets kinda little in comparison. Don't let yourself ever forget the important truth of the gospel. It's your lifeline. It's your salvation. It's your only hope and all the hope in the world.

A FIGHT TO THE FINISH

Check out how Eugene Peterson puts this section of Paul's letter to the Ephesians in his paraphrase of the Bible called *The Message*:

And that about wraps it up. God is strong, and he wants you strong. So take everything the Master has set out for you, well-made weapons of the best materials. And put them to use so you will be able to stand up to everything the Devil throws your way. This is no afternoon athletic contest that we'll walk away from and forget about in a couple of hours. This is for keeps, a life-or-death fight to the finish against the Devil and all his angels.

Be prepared. You're up against far more than you can handle on your own. Take all the help you can get, every weapon God has issued, so that when it's all over but the shouting you'll still be on your feet. Truth, righteousness, peace, faith, and salvation are more than words. Learn how to apply them. You'll need them throughout your life. God's Word is an indispensable weapon. In the same way, prayer is essential in this ongoing warfare. Pray hard and long. Pray for your brothers and sisters. Keep your eyes open. Keep each other's spirits up so that no one falls behind or drops out.

Ephesians 6:10–18 Message Paraphrase

RELENTLESS

> You're blessed when you're at the end of your rope. With less of you there is more of God and his rule.
>
> Matthew 5:3, *The Message Paraphrase*

When it comes to mean, you can try lots of ways to win over a Mean Girl. But one thing you have to consider is that you might never, ever win her over. That doesn't mean you failed; it just means that she's not ready. Changing her isn't your job, but loving your enemies and forgiving people is. When a soul loves and forgives, it soars to freedom on wings like an eagle's. But a soul bound to revenge and bitterness sinks to the depths of the sea and lives forever bound by the chains of self.

So when it comes to your Mean Girl, focus on what you are to do instead of what you think she should do or become. Don't look for an outcome; just keep your eye on the process of you becoming the woman you were made to be. How will you ever prove who you are? How will you ever prove your strength if you don't go through tough battles in life? Each attack that you live through and, more than that, *love* through, is a victory for your soul. Think of your soul like a big round diamond in the rough, and imagine that each blow that she throws at you and you absorb rather than throw back is hitting the diamond and knocking off another chunk of black carbon. As you grow, your diamond will become more and more brilliant as the dull pieces are chipped away to reveal the shimmering pure center.

You are a girl with power. You are a free spirit who has the willpower and ability to choose your destiny. A road paved with bitterness and resentment will lead you to a life of depression and agony. But if you pave your road with hope and love, your spirit will soar, and you will rise above the rest as a daughter of the

King. Your strength of spirit will be obvious to everyone. They will applaud you, they will want to be around you, and they will want to be like you. Only those who have suffered great loss truly are prepared to lead the rest of us to victory. Only those who have felt the flaming arrows of anger and jealousy and not returned a single one are fully prepared to serve a living King.

Only those who have felt the

flaming arrows of anger and jealousy and not returned a single one

are prepared to serve a living King.

Your goal in life should not be to change evil people and not to stop their attacks, but to follow the King. If you keep your eye on the prize instead of on the enemy, you will change more hearts and impact more people than you ever could with your own strength. If your most important goal is to love the King and to know him more, then take this attack from the enemy as a call for a step *toward* God, not away from him. Remember, the enemy loses in the end. Read the book called Revelation, 'cuz it is a real revelation—he loses. It's right there in the 20th chapter, 10th verse: LOSER. So your tormentors are inconsequential in the grand scheme of things. Their only real purpose is to drive you either closer to or farther from God. Which will it be? Will you whine, worry, fret, fear, and seek revenge, or will you rise above, dismiss the enemy and his powerlessness, and surround yourself with praises for your King? The choice is yours, my sister. Choose wisely.

"You're **blessed** when you're at the end of your rope. With less of you there is more of God and his rule. You're blessed when you feel you've lost what is most dear to you. Only then can you be embraced by the One most dear to you. You're blessed when you're content with just who you are—no more, no less. That's the moment you find yourselves proud owners of everything that can't be bought. . . . You're blessed **when you care**. At the moment of being 'care-full,' you find yourselves cared for. . . . You're blessed when you can show people how to cooperate instead of compete or fight. That's when you discover who you really are, and your place in God's family. You're blessed when your commitment to God provokes persecution. The persecution drives you even deeper into God's kingdom. Not only that—count yourselves **blessed every time people put you down** or throw you out or speak lies about you to discredit me. What it means is that the truth is too close for comfort and they are uncomfortable. You can be glad when that happens—give a cheer, even!—for though they don't like it, I do! And all heaven applauds."

Matthew 5:3–5, 7, 9–12, THE MESSAGE

[For my determined purpose is] that I may know Him [that I may progressively become more deeply and intimately acquainted with Him, perceiving and recognizing and understanding the wonders of His Person more strongly and more clearly], and that I may in that same way come to know the power outflowing from His resurrection [which it exerts over believers], and that I may so share His sufferings as to be continually transformed [in spirit into His likeness even] to His death.

Philippians 3:10 AMP

ENDING
MEAN

GETTING THE MEAN OUT OF YOUR CIRCLE

Now that we've worked the mean out of you, let's take a look at your circle. How can you help to get the mean out? First let me just say congrats on making it this far and congrats on the changes you're putting yourself through. It's hard work, this sanctification stuff, setting yourself apart for obedience to God's Word. But in the end the payoff is supreme. God doesn't want you to stop with yourself, though. No, he wants you to spread the love. All over the Bible we are called to make disciples. To lead others to repentance. I bet you never really knew how you fit into that whole scene. Well, now you do. It's as simple as helping other girls learn what you've learned and helping your school or workplace to become a mean-free zone.

Imagine if no girl ever had to feel the sting of rejection or hatred. Imagine a place where God's Word reigned supreme. I know, that seems like a stretch, because even if you go to Christian school or work at a Christian business, people still forget to live like Christians.

I believe that your desire, just like mine, is to follow God's teachings and to prove to yourself and to him that you trust him. And because of that, your life is going to change. Lucky for us, God never gives up on us. Even though we might have messed up in the past, he never throws his hands up in the air and walks away. He is ready to help us the moment we are ready to come back to him and trust him.

You might have been a Mean Girl in the past, or maybe you were just a girl who thought it was okay to get even. Either way, now is your chance to change. And when you've begun the change in yourself, then and only then can you begin to change the world around you. With these newfound truths and precepts you have the ability, through the Holy Spirit, to change not just yourself but your entire circle. One of my favorite quotes for reaching out to others is from the ancient book of Proverbs 24:11–12:

> Rescue those being led away to death; hold back those staggering toward slaughter. If you say, "But we knew nothing about this," does not he who weighs the heart perceive it? Does not he who guards your life know it? Will he not repay each person according to what he has done?

Now is your chance to rescue those who are staggering toward slaughter. If you don't do something to help the state of girls, do you expect God to look the other way? He has told you what he requires of you, and now you cannot say, "But we knew nothing about this." Until today you might not have known what was expected of you when it comes to Mean Girls, but now you do, so now you are responsible for doing what you can to change your reactions to them and even to help change the reactions of others in your group and in your school. After all, if you don't do something, who will? You were made for a time such as this. You were made to rise above the pettiness of the world and whatever the outcome, whatever the response, you can know that God is looking down at you and saying, "Well done, good and faithful servant" (Matthew 25:21). No matter what the outcome of our obedience on earth, we know that the outcome in heaven is blessings from him. God doesn't let your obedience go unrewarded.

I believe that today God is asking all of us to take back the feminine gender from the enemy. I believe he wants to start with you and your generation, to make you who you were intended to be: imitators of Christ, not the world. And I also believe that he has enlisted you as his soldier in this holy war. As a soldier you will need your orders and your weapons. So if you are ready, let's dive into defeating the mean.

PRAY THE MEAN OUT OF YOUR CIRCLE

You don't have the power to change people, but you do have the power to pray to the God who can. If you have allowed God to start cleaning you up to be holy in how you deal with Mean Girls yourself, then you can start to work toward cleaning up your school spiritually. A lot of what you've learned in this book will set you on the road to healing your circle, but if you want to take it a step further, think about the fact that there is power in numbers. Jesus said,

> Again, I tell you that if two of you on earth agree about anything you ask for, it will be done for you by my Father in heaven.
>
> Matthew 18:19

So what does prayer look like in your circle? Let me first start by telling you what it doesn't look like:

1. No gossip. Prayer is not an opp to gossip. Don't use your prayer time to tell other girls the terrible things that are going on. Don't mention them. Your job isn't to spread more gossip; it's to stop it. So no talking about what bad things other girls are doing.

2. No cliques. If your prayer group becomes a clique, you are way off. No one who is spiritually serious should be excluded, or you'll be behaving just like the rest of those Mean Girls.

3. Don't give up if you don't see a change. Remember, God's timing is flawless. He might not do things according to your time frame, but it isn't your job to care about that. If you pray only because you demand results, your prayer will soon die because you won't be getting your way. Prayer is just as much about changing you and your spirit as it is about changing the object of prayer. So go to God in faith and rest in the fact that whatever the outcome, all is well. Pray, "Your will be done on earth as it is in heaven" (Matthew 6:10).

Now that we've gone through the don't-do list, let's think about some ways that you can use prayer to improve the female community around you:

1. Pray Scripture. The Bible is full of truth, and that truth spoken out loud is extremely powerful. Use God's Word to tell him what you want for your Mean Girl. Pray for your school, your home, your work, or wherever you deal with meanness. You'll find tons of Scriptures throughout this book, so check them out and find some of your own.

2. Memory verse. Take it a step further and decide on a memory verse or two that each of you will learn and carry with you. Put it on your day planner, bathroom mirror, and cell phone. Memorize it and live it. (Check out the book of Proverbs 7:1–3.)

3. Faith in action. James tells us that faith without action is dead (see James 2:17). So make it a part of your ritual to put into practice the things you pray for. As James Allen said, "Not what he wishes and prays for does a man get, but what he justly earns. His wishes and prayers are only gratified and answered when they harmonize with his thoughts and actions." Figure out ways to put verses into action. Here are some to get you started:

   a. Verse: "Do not conform any longer to the pattern of this world, but be transformed by the renewing of your mind. Then you will be able to test and approve what God's will is—his good, pleasing and perfect will" (Romans 12:2).

Action: Change the way you think. Renew your mind to think like God and help the rest of your group to do the same. Think of every girl you meet as a child of God. See her how he sees her. That means that you will risk caring for her. If a Mean Girl is attacking another girl, come to her aid. Be there for her. Take her away from the attack or say something nice about her. When you think about people differently it's much easier to act upon God's Word.

b. Verse: "If you confess with your mouth, 'Jesus is Lord,' and believe in your heart that God raised him from the dead, you will be saved" (Romans 10:9).

Action: Tell girls about the amazing life and death of your Savior. Love them enough to want to save them from the gates of hell.

c. Verse: "For God did not give us a spirit of timidity, but a spirit of power, of love and of self-discipline" (2 Timothy 1:7).

Action: Dare to make friends with the odd girl out—the one no one quite gets or even wants to be around. Become her friend.

d. Verse: "A generous man will himself be blessed, for he shares his food with the poor" (Proverbs 22:9).

Action: Volunteer in your community or, if you have extra cash, talk to a teacher, boss, or pastor about giving money anonymously to people in your circle who need it.

e. Verse: "A cheerful heart is good medicine, but a crushed spirit dries up the bones" (Proverbs 17:22).

Action: Be happy. A smile can be a great gift to give someone, especially if they are dealing with Mean Girls. Some people might go a whole week without seeing anyone smile at them. Believe God's Word and give from it generously.

4. Bible study. Go through a *Mean Girls* Bible study with your friends, mom, sister, or whoever. Start to spread the news to this hungry planet about a life lived for God and free of mean. See **nomoremean.com** or **iFuse.com** for more info.

5. The GG. Gather a group of girls to sign the God Girl Contract at the end of this book, and then hold each other accountable to your promise.

LEAVE NO MEAN GIRL BEHIND
(FOR ADVANCED READERS ONLY)

Here is the challenge and battle cry for those of you who feel you have this down: leave no Mean Girl behind! Let's rescue them one by one. Let's refuse to fan the flame of their anger, and instead let's nurture the love of their hearts. This might be the hardest thing you've ever done, but the rewards can be amazing.

Imagine a world where girls don't fight each other and where they aren't consumed with getting even or making life miserable for girls who have more than them. It seems like a pipe dream, I know, but I believe that if every girl reading this book could infect two other girls with this message, and those two could infect two more, and so on and so on, we could significantly change a generation of females.

This is something that has yet to be done. Right now, girls are mean in every generation. But I believe this is something the Holy Spirit wants from us, especially as the family of believers. All of his words point to this. Imagine if your sisterhood of believers were all God Girls and we didn't have a Mean Girl among us. Think how that would look to the outside world. Girls would really want to know more about this Christ that makes girls happy and fulfilled. So your challenge, should you choose to accept it, is to infect at least two other girls with this message and encourage them to do the same.

Log on to **nomoremean.com** or **iFuse.com** to find more girls who are taking the Mean Girl challenge. Compare notes. Start a revolution! Help make your generation the first generation of girls who aren't Mean Girls.

To hook up with more girls looking to put an end to Mean Girls, go to our online social at **iFuse.com.**

CHOOSING CHRIST

As you should have figured out by now, none of this is possible without God. But there is a bonus: his love for you is about more than just saving you from the Mean Girl—it's about saving you too. If you want hope and purpose in your life, you will find it all when you get to know God. And if you don't know him right now, here is your chance. If you are tired of living life under your own power without all of these assurances that you've read about, then pray this simple prayer right now and you will get this life-changing power absolutely free.

Dear God, I thought I knew who you were but I don't think I ever did. I have been living my life the way I wanted, and I'm not doing such a good job. I know that I can't do it by myself anymore. I need you. I want you. I confess that I've done most of it all wrong, and now I want to do it right. I trust what the Bible says about you, and I want to be obedient to it. I trust you to save me and to give me eternal life. I believe that Christ died for me on the cross so that my sins could be forgiven if I just believe. So today, God, I tell you that I accept Christ as my Savior and want to make him Lord of my life. Thank you for loving me. I love you, Lord. Amen.

If you confess with your mouth that Jesus is Lord and believe in your heart that God raised him from the dead, you will be saved. For with the heart one believes and is justified, and with the mouth one confesses and is saved.

Romans 10:9–10

THE GOD GIRL (GG)

The antithesis of giving thanks is grumbling. The grumblers
live in state of self-induced stress.

—Brennan Manning

Let me ask you this: So check out what makes you mean-free
and decide today if that's the kind of life you want.

The big question: what is the opposite of the Mean Girl? As
I racked my brain to try to figure out what it is, my first thought
was, well, of course, it's the nice girl. But "nice girl" has come to
be kind of a bad term, almost an insult. So I kept thinking. Finally
I said to myself, a *God Girl* is the complete opposite of a Mean
Girl. The God Girl is a good friend. She is obedient to her Father.
So from now on, the opposite of the MG is the GG.

My call to you is to decide right now to be a God Girl. Choose
to be godly and good over mean. Do you think God smiles when
you are mean, or when you are good? If you want to live by his
Word, then you have no choice but to drop the mean scene and
pick up the good vibe. Become an all-new God Girl. If you want
to be a good friend and a godly girl, then look over this list and
start learning and practicing what GGs do.

1. *GGs aren't defensive.* GGs can be confronted with stuff
   without flipping out. After all, it isn't all about you; it's all
   about loving the Lord your God with all your heart, soul, and
   mind and loving your neighbor as yourself. "*Jesus replied,*
   '*You must love the Lord your God with all your heart, all
   your soul, and all your mind.' This is the first and greatest
   commandment. A second is equally important: 'Love your
   neighbor as yourself.'*" (Matthew 22:37–39 NLT). If you

truly want to grow to be a better person, you'll be open to learning more about yourself. Face it, you're too close to yourself to see where you need, shall we say, improvements. No one can ever see all their own faults; that's why God gave us friends. Just like iron sharpens iron, friends make each other sharper and more useful.

2. *GGs don't gossip.* Gossip—God hates it (see Leviticus 19:16). It's yucky. Painful. Vicious. Uncalled-for. GGs avoid gossip because God detests it, period, the end. Don't let gossip rule your heart. Just say no.

3. *GGs don't seek revenge.* Revenge is a sin. It's taking what's God's. He is the only one with the power of punishment, not you. Don't take over God's role and try to be God in your relationships. Danger. Bad territory to mess around in.

4. *GGs are spiritual, not religious.* You have a relationship with a living and breathing being, Jesus Christ, not with a list of rules and regulations. The moment you step away from Christ and solely into a list of dos and don'ts is the moment it gets a lot easier to be a Mean Girl.

5. *GGs aren't afraid to look stupid.* Who are you trying to please? God or people? If you are trying to please people, you'll freak out if someone sees you do something stupid. But I believe you would rather please God than people, so don't be afraid to look stupid. It's not about appearances but about who you are. Laugh at yourself. Don't worry about your image as much as you focus on loving others.

6. *GGs care for others.* If Christ is your example, then check him out. He wasn't all about his needs; he was all about others. He worked when he was tired, and he healed when he was worn out. He gave to others who could do nothing

for him. If you care for others, you will never be called a Mean Girl.

7. *GGs hold each other accountable.* In Revelation 2:4, 14, and 20, you will find that Jesus held the church accountable for its actions. As friends, we keep each other in check. A GG knows that it's healthy to tell each other the truth in love. She isn't afraid to confront her friend and to talk things out.

8. *GGs forgive.* Check out 1 Corinthians chapter 13, verse 5. God forgives, therefore God Girls forgive. If you want to imitate Christ, forgiveness is your first action item. No forgiveness from you, no forgiveness *for* you. "*If you forgive those who sin against you, your heavenly Father will forgive you*" (Matthew 6:14 NLT).

9. *GGs are happy for the wins of their friends.* It doesn't have to be all about you. You want others to be happy, and when they are, you are. GGs don't feel bad when other people win, because after all, it isn't all about you.

10. *GGs leave others feeling good about themselves.* GGs aren't in it for their own glory. They truly care about others, so when they are with people, people feel the love. Don't leave your friends feeling worse than when they started talking to you. Care about them and you will be a true GG.

11. *GGs have good friends.* In order to be the GG you want to be, you need to spend most of your time with other GGs. They'll rub off on you, and you can hold each other accountable to goodness. "Can two people walk together without agreeing on the direction?" (That's wisdom from the book of Amos, chapter 3, verse 3 NLT.)

If you agree with that list and want to start today to live it, then sign the God Girl Contract at the end of this book. It's a contract between you and God to be signed in the presence of other sisters in Christ. This is your chance to commit yourself to honoring him no matter what. It's also your chance to take a stand and turn back the tide of Mean Girls. With each girl who signs the contract, we are one girl closer to changing the feminine species from mean to faithful. This is not a contract to take lightly. Hey, it isn't a task to take lightly. Honoring God never is. So before you sign it, be sure you mean it. Search your heart and determine if you are ready to follow Christ's heart and to give up pleasing yourself. Frankly, I believe it is your only choice if you want to call yourself a follower of the Messiah. Are you ready?

THE GOD GIRL CONTRACT

In the last chapter, "The God Girl," I told you what a GG is. If you agree with that list and want to start today to live it, then here's the next step: the God Girl Contract. This is a contract between you and God to be signed in the presence of other sisters in Christ. Agree to hold each other accountable to it. Use the verses that go with it as a memory verse list to keep you on track. You can cut this contract out and keep it with you or hang it somewhere you'll see it to help you remember your commitment. And you can go to **nomoremean.com** for a downloadable contract if you need copies for all your GG friends. Are you ready to be mean-free forever?

Before you sign, pray this prayer:

Father God, I am so much like Paul, who said, "What I don't understand about myself is that I decide one way, but then I act another, doing things I absolutely despise. . . . For if I know the law but still can't keep it, and if the power of sin within me keeps sabotaging my best intentions, I obviously need help! I realize that I don't have what it takes. I can will it, but I can't do it. I decide to do good, but I don't really do it; I decide not to do bad, but then I do it anyway. . . . Something has gone wrong deep within me and gets the better of me every time" (Romans 7:15–20, The Message paraphrase). I don't like this side of me, but I know it exists, and because of that I say thank you for Jesus and his death on the cross. I am not worthy, but I accept the gift of salvation as a free one that I don't have to do anything for other than to say yes. I'm tired of using all my energy to say no to sin, so I'd rather say yes to you. Your Word says I can't live a sinless and blameless life, so instead of concentrating on the bad, I will concentrate on saying yes to you and allow you to say no to sin for me.

Father, I want to find out what pleases you and do it. In this book I have read about many things that you want us to do, and now I am ready to do them. So today I commit to this list in front of you and my sisters. Help me keep my commitment. Thank you that you always do help me in my weakness. Amen.

MY GOD GIRL CONTRACT

I, _____ of _____ enter into this contract on this month and day of _____, 20__, for the purpose of glorifying God with my heart, mind, and actions. To this end I commit to take the following steps to make my little circle of this world a better place for all girls.

By signing this contract, I agree to the following conditions:

1. **I will not be defensive.** "When they hurled their insults at him, he did not retaliate; when he suffered, he made no threats. Instead, he entrusted himself to him who judges justly" (1 Peter 2:23).
2. **I will not gossip.** "Don't pass on malicious gossip" (Exodus 23:1 Message).
3. **I will not seek revenge.** "Do not take revenge, my friends, but leave room for God's wrath, for it is written: 'It is mine to avenge; I will repay,' says the Lord" (Romans 12:19).
4. **I will be gentle of spirit, not religious and legalistic.** "[Your beauty] should be . . . the unfading beauty of a gentle and quiet spirit, which is of great worth in God's sight" (1 Peter 3:4).
5. **I will laugh at myself.** "Obviously, I'm not trying to be a people pleaser! No, I am trying to please God. If I were still trying to please people, I would not be Christ's servant" (Galatians 1:10 NLT).
6. **I will care for others.** "Love never gives up. Love cares more for others than for self" (1 Corinthians 13:4 Message).

7 **I will hold other GGs accountable.** "Share each other's troubles and problems, and in this way obey the law of Christ" (Galatians 6:2 NLT).

8. **I will forgive.** "If you forgive those who sin against you, your heavenly Father will forgive you" (Matthew 6:14 NLT).

9. **I will be happy when other girls win.** Love "doesn't revel when others grovel, takes pleasure in the flowering of truth, puts up with anything, trusts God always, always looks for the best, never looks back, but keeps going to the end" (1 Corinthians 13:6–7 Message).

10. **I will do all I can to leave others feeling good about themselves.** "Watch the way you talk. Let nothing foul or dirty come out of your mouth. Say only what helps, each word a gift" (Ephesians 4:29 Message).

_____

(your name)

life + faith + love + truth

Hayley DiMarco's Page

Hayley DiMarco
Female
Nashville, TN, United States
+ Add as friend
✉ Send a Message
⁂ Share

Latest Activity

Hayley DiMarco left a comment for Brittany
1 day ago

Erin left a comment for Hayley DiMarco
1 day ago

Taylor and Hayley DiMarco are now friends

1 day ago

Hayley DiMarco added the blog post 'Sexy Fashion Fixes'
1 day ago

Hayley DiMarco left a comment for Erin
1 day ago

Hayley DiMarco left a comment for Katie
1 day ago

Hayley DiMarco is chief creative officer and founder of Hungry Planet, where she writes and creates cutting-edge books that connect with the multitasking mindset. She has written and co-written numerous bestselling books for both teens and adults, including *Dateable*, *Mean Girls*, *Sexy Girls*, and *Technical Virgin*. She and her husband, Michael, live in Nashville, Tennessee.

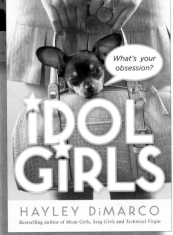

Feed Yourself Some Truth with PB&J!

The **P**ocket **B**ible study **&** **J**ournal series includes studies on . . .

Dating
Mean
Hotness
Sex

Whether you're a student or a youth leader, don't miss:

- **iFuse.com**: sign up your group in the new social community from HP!

- **HungryPlanet.tv**: download videos of Hayley introducing each section of the PB & J series

- **HungryPlanet.net**: download free leader's guides

R Revell
a division of Baker Publishing Group
www.revellbooks.com

www.hungryplanet.net